T0285660

WEALTH IN THE KEY OF LIFE

WEALTH IN THE KEY OF LIFE

FINDING YOUR FINANCIAL HARMONY

PRESTON D. CHERRY

WILEY

Published by John Wiley & Sons, Inc., Hoboken, New Jersey.

Published simultaneously in Canada.

For general information on our other products and services or for technical support, please contact our Customer Care Department within the United States at (800) 762-2974, outside the United States at (317) 572-3993 or fax (317) 572-4002.

Wiley also publishes its books in a variety of electronic formats. Some content that appears in print may not be available in electronic formats. For more information about Wiley products, visit our web site at www.wiley.com.

Library of Congress Cataloging-in-Publication Data is Available:

ISBN 9781394268665 (Cloth)
ISBN 9781394268672 (ePDF)
ISBN 9781394268689 (epub)

Cover Design: Wiley
Cover Image: © Adrian/Adobe Stock Photos
Author Photo: Courtesy of the Author

SKY10089712_110124

CONTENTS

CONTENTS

ACKNOWLEDGMENTS

I firmly believe people are not self-made even if they didn't receive an inheritance. Yes, hard work and choices matter, and so do access and resources, which include living and post-life transfers – financial and otherwise. Why does that matter? Because people have believed and supported me throughout my journey, I'm grateful for their investment.

You'll always hear me say, "Faith as you define it" because I respect people having their own relationship with Faith. My first acknowledgment is God. He is the most merciful and most gracious, and all praise be to God. There are so many instances in my life where He brought me exactly what I needed and, many times, what I wanted into my life. I thank God for accepting my imperfections, forgiving my transgressions, and allowing me to maximize myself and others with what He has given me.

Next, I want to thank my parents, Charles Jr. and Carla Cherry. They gave my sister and me the greatest gifts you can give human beings: love, self-worth, and self-value. These are the compoundable assets I often speak of, and I received them and the ideas from them. Their intentional decisions to invest in us gave us the opportunities we have now, either directly or indirectly. Also, their wisdom and example of love and life can't be overstated. I received my confidence to be myself, assuredness in life's decisions, leadership, personal style, and more from my father. I received the gift of humanity from my mother. I received *all* my financial psychology intuition and intelligence from her – vulnerability, compassion, courage, willingness, and wanting to be understood. I could go on, but I tell them this stuff every chance I get. Pops and Mother dear, I love and appreciate you more than you know. Thank you.

Next are my sister, brother-in-law (whom I call my *brother*), and beloved niece – Jennifer, Ryan, and Maddison. My sister and I are the late-stage Millennials and Gen Xers who lived the Latchkey Kid life, coming home after school to a household with only us young people until our parents came home from work. We have a special bond of brother-sisterhood that only we can understand, and we share countless life experiences, memories, and lessons that we carry forever – along with a library of movie quotes! My brother, Ryan, is a fantastic husband and father, and as a brother to a sister, there's no one better I could have chosen for my sister. He's *that* dude, and he's a true friend of mine. Then there's my Maddie Mae! Wow, this little girl, now a young woman, was part of saving my life and helping me stay in my willingness to change and on a transformational journey. Maddison is a true joy, a kindred spirit filled with talent and a big heart. Jennifer, Ryan, and Maddison, I love you dearly. Thank you.

Everyone in this acknowledgment is valued in their unique way. There's a special and indescribable place for wife, friend, soul mate, and business partner Dr. Eiman Osseilan-Cherry and our recently born son, Laith. I met Eiman at Texas Tech University while pursuing our personal financial planning degrees. That's relevant because, when I entered that pursuit and based on previous life experiences, I concluded that I wasn't going to pursue or meet, by chance, anyone I could consider my life partner. God made sure I was wrong and blessed me with a person who is so right for me – and I am forever grateful! Eiman and I have a story that can fill another book. Just know that I knew from the start I wanted to spend my life with her, and I greatly appreciate how she has believed and supported me and helped lead our family on how to be a phenomenal and brave person and to pursue your dreams on your own path. Eiman, "thank you" doesn't fully say what I need it to, but thank you for taking life's journey with me. First, you and I, and now us with a son. Thank you, and I love you beyond and forever! And to my Saudi family – the Osseilan family – thank you for loving me and supporting me, Eiman, and now Laith to thrive in life with love. I appreciate how God has blessed me with two families in different places on this Earth; our families are connected through God's grace. Thank you for everything.

Laith, my boy, all of this work and input placed into me is now for you. God blessed me (us) with you at the perfect time in life. I wanted you earlier in life, but God knows best. I am deeply connected with you and aim to try my best daily – you are my purpose. One day, you will read this book and these acknowledgments and see that I've been blessed with all this human capital investment and spiritual guidance from God. Outside of me (us) telling you, you have a public source here. I love you with a love I've never experienced. I am someone's son, but I've never been someone's father. I am yours. I love you!

A special shout-out to my Houston and Kansas City families, the former being my hometown and the latter my birth town. To my Kansas City family – rest assured, some of our family dynamics are the same for many families worldwide. Some are to be celebrated and transferred; others need healing and change. Let's continue to grow. Thank you to my grandparents Charles Sr. and Cleo Cherry, Uncle Chris, Aunt Gwen, and all the Wesley, Lewis, and Williams families. Houston, you hold a special place in my heart for how I came up and developed. Thank you to all my Houston friends, colleagues, and associates. You know who you are. H-town!

My dear friends, mentors, and colleagues. My best friend, Dr. Ajamu Loving – much love, my brother; there are no words for how much I feel blessed to have you as a friend. My dear friend Chauncey Bogan, I value our friendship more than you know. Thank you, and I love you. Raheem Merritt and family, I love you, you already know. Sean Richards and the Richards family, having a family and friends to grow up with and through life is immeasurable. I thank you and love you.

When I say no one is self-made, this entire acknowledgment section is proof of that. Here are cheers to more of my mentors, colleagues, and friends who have been invaluable to my life. Dr. Jan Jasper, Lazetta Rainey Braxton, Saundra Davis, Dr. Freddie Richards, Dr. Vickie Hampton, Dr. Bill Gustafson, Dr. Dorothy Durband, Dr. Mitzi Lauderdale, Deena Katz, Harold Evensky, Steve Sanduski, Anthony Stich, Dr. Mark and Melissa Evers, Dr. Philip Gibson, Dr. Sarah Asebedo, Jamie Hopkins, Caleb Silver, Dr. Nathan Harness, Dr. Craig Lemoine, Christine Benz, Chloe Moore, Jim Pavia, Angela Moore, Jonathan Jones, Dominique Henderson, Mark Tibergien, Walter Booker, Dr. Meg Lurtz, Dr. Alex Melkumian, Emlen-Miles Mattingly, Rickie Taylor, David Linton, Roz Davis, Katie Cullen, Micheal Lane, Wayne Resch, Sherri Trombley, Trudy Turner, Victor Jones, Dean Mathew Dornbush, Cordero and Erin Barkley, Josh Brown, Jarvis Johnson, "Mike D.," Sean and Brenda Miller, Texas Tech School of Financial Planning, Prairie View A&M University, Cypress, Texas, Cy-Fair High School, Financial Therapy Association, CFP Board, Financial Planning Association, AFCPE, CNBC, Schwab Network, the Charles Schwab Foundation, Schwab Advisor Services, the University of Wisconsin of Green Bay, and all students I've had the pleasure of teaching.

I've always wanted to be a writer, and being an author with a major publisher is a dream. A few of the people who helped to spearhead introductions and ideas were Ellen Rogin, Brian Portnoy, Suzzane Siracuse, Lynnette-Khalfani Cox, and Earl Cox. Speaking of publishers, I want to thank Judith Newlin, Vithusha Rameshan, and the Wiley team. Thank you for believing in my voice and vision and for your support.

I promise I could list hundreds of others in these acknowledgments; if I missed you, please blame my mind and not my heart and know that I cherish your contribution and our relationship.

To all the readers of this book, clients, and followers of my contributions to the world – my mission is to advance the human condition through personal finance and life testimony – thank you for allowing me to be a part of your life through this book, and I hope it helps in some way. Here's to you finding your *Wealth in the Key of Life*!

INTRODUCTION

A PERSONAL JOURNEY TO HOLISTIC WEALTH: FROM BANKRUPTCY TO BALANCE

I f you drive, you know how your car feels when the front-end alignment is out of whack. The car drifts left or right and becomes hard to steer, leaving you powerless. Instead of steering the car where you want it to go, your car controls your course. Then you repair your car, aligning it to achieve your desired driving experience so it can safely take you to your destination. Now, you and the car are working harmoniously on your travel journey. For several years, my life and money felt like a car with its front end out of alignment, steering me off course and leaving me with no control.

Excessively drinking alcohol to addiction nearly killed me. The journey through alcoholism also saved my life. The resilience to survive the trial helped me figure out what I didn't want to do any longer and unlocked what I did want to do. Moving from trial to triumph was not easy or linear, but the transformation and resulting transition needed first simply to start. Personal transformation can start with a trial event or a triumphant event; the flashpoint moment is unique to the individual. The key to transformation is using that moment to reflect upon where you are and where you want to go and using that discovery as motivation to change your course. The motivation serves as an inspiration to avoid or to work through pain points to achieve your version of flourishing.

YOUR STORY GIVES YOUR FREEDOM

Your stories are your gateway to achieving financial freedom and the life you envision. When you tap into your story, you tap into your money. Let me tell you mine; I hope you find encouragement to embrace yours.

I graduated with a master's in personal financial planning from Texas Tech in the winter of 2006, and from 2007 to 2008, I thrived. I secured two career-defining positions, new money heights, and personal accomplishments. The first was a respectably high salary for my life stage, and I felt secure enough to purchase a condo. The second position was a breakthrough career position with a generous six-figure compensation package with junior executive–type benefits like signing and performance bonuses, relocation expenses, and home-selling subsidies. I was in my late twenties and felt like I was progressing ahead of my expected personal life and money schedule.

The next seven years were what I call the "fog" years. I embarrassingly lost that second career position quickly, followed by losing the condo, ultimately leading me to bankruptcy. My financial regret is that I had a well-off tenant in their early 60s who paid rent in six-month installments in advance, and the condo had a prime location, so I missed out on real estate income and appreciation. But that's not the worst of it; I lost sight of my aspirational life – an essential theme to life and money prosperity in this book. The sting of failure brought by the guilt and shame of self-destruction engulfed me. Wasting the gift of precious time coupled with not maximizing life's opportunities fueled an onslaught of self-medication at best, abuse or addiction at worst.

Craving mind- and spirit-altering substances transforms into chemical dependency. Artificial chemicals that connect with the brain's natural chemicals devilishly capture reason, which uncontrollably replaces reality with an alternative state of being: a false, yet at times euphorically calm state of well-being that is unsustainable. There was never going to be enough to feed my subsidized state that froze my inner conflicts and current issues so that my soul could function warmly. The only two outcomes were to admit and address or continue toward a certain death. Reaching this conclusion and finding what was killing me should have been the worst, but it wasn't.

Much worse was discovering that a complete disconnect from my values, a total loss of self-identity and worth, and lacking the hope of ever understanding and healing my pain was killing me more than the substances. I didn't know that traveling a pathway toward rock bottom would lead me to admit I was sparking a process to pursue the freedom to transform and transition to the life I want. You'll read how admitting during your Honest Self-Audit kicks off finding the information you need to guide the senses and strategy of your financial life plan.

MOVING FROM DARK TO LIGHT

I was doing well professionally, but I was dying personally. How I used my lifestyle to cope led my money down the drain. My life and finances were markedly disconnected, displaying no concurrent partnership. My money financed reactions to my life; I did not allow my life to direct the purpose of my money.

During the "fog years," the clouds during the day and the dark of night felt good because the weather matched my soul. I was comfortable there – until I wasn't. The old-schoolers would say I was "broke, busted, dusted, and disgusted!" I was ready for the sunshine to shed light on me, for reflection, and in me for inspiration. I was ready for change. It was one of my final benders that moved me from darkness to light.

Outside my condo, there was a streetlight for a transit stop, which shone through my window at night, even with the blinds drawn. I required blackout curtains, which I did not have, to achieve pitch-black darkness. So the room was dark but not pitch dark. I arrived home around 4:00 a.m., worn out from drunkenness. After entering, I dropped to the floor, crawled to my bedroom, and lay on my back. I was exhausted not just from that night but from life. I did not want to end my life, but had it ended at that moment, I wouldn't have minded. Figuratively, I felt dead.

Because the streetlight was coming through the window, the room wasn't dark enough to match the darkness inside of my soul. I didn't have enough coordination to walk, so I crawled to the windowless bathroom so I could achieve darker darkness, so I could be more comfortable in my guilt and shame.

There was a crack at the bottom of the bathroom door, letting light inside. Spread out on the floor, I didn't think I was worthy of the sliver of light, so I had to find a darker place to feel more comfortable. I crawled into the closet and shut the door from the inside. The bottom of the closet door gripped the carpet tight, letting in no light; I found that I required it to be even darker still. I parted the clothes and crawled behind them into a corner, finally achieving the darkness and emptiness of my self-worth and value. At this moment, I realized what I didn't want to do and what I wanted to do; I wanted more light, and I wanted more life – the life I envisioned.

FINDING LIFE MONEY BALANCE

With tears of desperation, I crawled from the closet toward the light and made two phone calls – one to my family and another for professional help. In that instant, I held my first Honest Self-Audit of my current situation, an essential step toward staging change and working toward sustainable action for an aspirational life.

After courageously and honestly admitting where I was, three things became apparent. First, my life situation was an emergency, with the current direction guaranteeing death. Second, my life was not where I wanted it to be. Third, I wanted to begin the journey of moving toward where I wanted to go. Unbeknownst to me, this was the moment when the Life Money Balance (LMB) philosophy was born.

LIFE MONEY BALANCE

Let your life lead your money, instead of your money leading your life; your life and money should work concurrently to create your life design.

The LMB system lets you partner your finances with the life you want. It requires engaging in vulnerable and bold steps and requires that you apply frameworks to help achieve life and money alignment by giving your money assignments to what you value most. The chapters in this book will help you apply LMB to your life's course.

It took years for me to recover. Step two in the Honest Self-Audit is to compassionately acknowledge how you feel about where you are, to process the Humanity of Money, clearing the path for healing that will jumpstart you toward action. Tea drinkers know there are types of tea for different moods and health conditions. Timely sipping your proper tea can promote better outcomes in your target area of health or mindset. There are "teas" ("T's") for your life and money flashpoints, life stages, milestones, and mindsets. Through faith, family, friends, and professional help, I was compelled to travel the Teas of Life – Trial, Triumph, Transformation, and Transition toward abundant living, full of thriving well-being and consistent wealth-building.

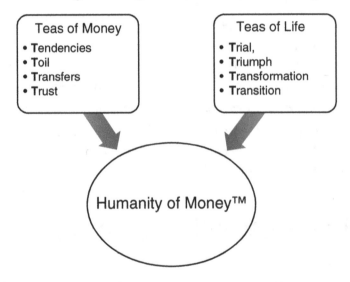

Self-investment started with first surviving to heal, then moving towards investments in thriving. Connecting my current and future self was essential to allowing my whole self to thrive across my life's course. In other words, my current self caring for my future self's preferences and purpose – and vice versa – is an essential element to the Integrated Life Stage Well-Being aspect of LMB, which we will discuss shortly.

I set on a course to transform my life's design and transition to the next stages of my life course. Through my testimony, I want others to gain the courage and vulnerability to live the life they want now and in their future. By using LMB, you can advance your human condition, pairing the Humanity of Money with sound financial insights to achieve what you value most.

FINDING HARMONY

Not addressing my emotional health was stunting my financial health at a great cost. The burden of not having answers to life's past and present was coming at the expense of my future, a price too expensive to pay. You can't find financial harmony with years of misalignment; your music notes of life will be off-key. The music of wealth has one producer – you – and your album will not flourish without your production.

The technical definitions of harmony are rooted in music and psychology. Harmonious music comes from combining notes playing together in chords, forming a holistic song that pleases your senses when you listen – heart, mind, and soul. Some songs sound like perfect harmony, and while there's no such thing as perfect, progress toward that perfection starts to sound like bliss. Harmony in psychology is a positive state of inner peace, calm, and balance within your social circles, between individuals, or within yourself.[1]

Much like mine, flashpoint moments require you to ask what life and financial notes will play together to create a song that will bring you peace, calm, and balance. These notes will allow you to build wealth, the key to living your aspirational life. Your life becomes the leader of your money, providing the connective glue that binds you to what you value most and a financial plan you will stick with. You find as much you don't want to do, so much as you do.

My "ahh" moment happened in 2016 after I came out of the fog. I asked myself, "Preston, what do you aspire to do?" The answer was "to help others advance their human condition, delivering financial education and advice through multiple platforms, such as an advice firm, global speaking, and academia." That alignment kicked off my aspirational journey, helping me assign my energy and dollars toward what I want to achieve. That's why I am writing this book. You, too, need to find and follow a framework to identify your ideal aspirational life, funded with wealth strategies that bring you fulfillment and help you flourish.

GRAB YOUR LIFE MONEY BALANCE

The LMB philosophy finds its inspirational roots in Dr. Martin Luther King's 1967 speech to junior high schoolers titled "What Is Your Life's Blueprint?" Dr. King asked,

> What is in your life's blueprint? This is the most important and crucial period of your lives. For what you do now and what you decide now may well determine which way your life shall go.

In 2018, I sought inspiration to create a guiding philosophy to help people find their *blueprint* as I had. How could I bridge my personal experiences, professional expertise, and academic knowledge to form a framework to achieve financial health and well-being?

I quickly discovered that your wealth-building and well-being journey is holistic.[2,3] You must consider your full human condition as part of your financial plan. Your financial health, well-being, self-worth, and self-value are your most compoundable and valuable assets. They combine your current and future selves to make your self-economy. The Six-A Alignment Framework uncovers and unlocks insights that inform the LMB Integrated Well-Being Approach that uniquely assigns your finances to flourishing domains across and within your life.

SIX-A ALIGNMENT FRAMEWORK

Six-A Alignment Framework™

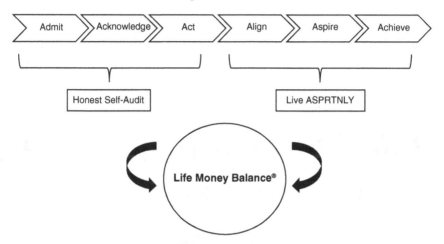

GRAB YOUR LIFE MONEY BALANCE

Life is a continuum of motion; the sky moves, and seasons change with the resilience to advance and adjust from one moment to the next. Your life has stages with unique characteristics, events, and meaning. Money works that way, too.

Across these life stages, your money evolves, and your finances find assignments that match what you value most. When your life and money are aligned, there is harmony. When they are misaligned, there is a conflict of contentment. LMB is a willingness to discover and dedicate yourself to an honest and transformational process that aligns life with money.

FIVE-POINT LIFE PLANNING PROCESS

Person + Preferences + Purpose + Points + Plan = Prosperity

The Six-A Alignment System informs the Five Point Life Planning Process that helps you live your LMB lifestyle as you envision – your *Wealth in the Key of Life.*

Approaching your financial life plan this way will help you discover your holistic self – past, present, and future. You will find understanding, unpack barriers, establish boundaries, inform your finances, build wealth, fund well-being, and set your course through the Sea of C's to gain clarity, confidence, and control.

Life Money Balance®
Integrated Life Stage Well-Being

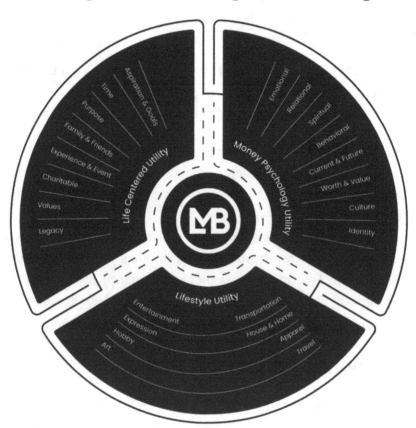

I want you to know that finding your financial harmony with the LMB philosophy is not just conceptual, meaningless words based on nothing.

These applications are based on theories from Nobel Prize–winning behavioral economists, widely accepted psychologists, and evidence-based empirical studies. This research combines financial planning and psychology to explore the various factors contributing to wealth and well-being.

The premise of LMB is rooted in a combination known as human-centered theories.

- Systems Theory
- Person-Centered Theory
- Humanistic Theory of Motivation
- Consumer Economic Theory
- Time Discounting

Systems Theory suggests that a whole is composed of interacting and interdependent parts that influence each other and the outcomes over time, where the sum benefit is greater than the benefit of the individual parts.[4] The LMB philosophy is a system of interactive domains at different life stages that continuously allows for change. Your household combines parts that work well together to empower the finances and fulfillment outcomes you want.

There are two motivation-based theories to achieve self-actualization or, in another way, their ideal or whole self. **Person-Centered Theory** says people have the self-motivation for change and find solutions to align their real and ideal selves.[5] The **Humanistic Theory** of Motivation, commonly referred to as Maslow's Hierarchy of Needs, claims that people are motivated to meet and move through a system of needs and wants to achieve self-actualization.[6]

Lastly, to throw in some finances, **Consumer Economic Theory** explains how people allocate their finances to purchase goods and services to maximize utility or well-being, considering their preferences, budget constraints, and choices over time.[7] Speaking of time, with

time discounting, people make choices about the value they place on the present and future. They use questions such as "Do you borrow resources from the future to fund the present?" or "Do you forgo pleasantries now to fund the future?" Some refer to the latter as delayed gratification. Know that too much of either could knock you off your course; we discuss this further in Chapters 6 and 8.[8]

What does the word-salad of theoretical sciences mean to you in plain-speak? It means that humans naturally want to combine their available resources to secure their best sense of wholeness and state of well-being to their liking. Our willingness to change and our decisions reflect our desire to achieve success in the way we define it.

Simply put, LMB *is* financial harmony through wealth-secured well-being, rooted in an evidence-based and philosophical theory approach, coupled with decades of life and financial planning experience. This approach lets your life lead your money, where your life and money work concurrently to achieve your life design. Everyone has a unique story, and stories inform their numbers. When your life and money are aligned, your money has assignments.

LIVING WEALTH IN THE KEY OF LIFE

Finding your financial harmony using the LMB philosophy is built on key theoretical elements. A central theme is that you are motivated to change, believing your preferences, identity, stories, and finances are unique, and you are worthy of abundance.

The LMB Wheel is a continuum of your self-economy that embraces domains of self-actualization and self-care. When you commit to unpacking your emotional intelligence areas and uncovering what you value most, you can assign your dollars to purchase additional units of what you value, increasing your well-being. The scientific word for well-being is *utility*. The LMB "keys of life" are the life you want – your utility, your well-being.

You get to choose what brings you increased well-being across time, making decisions with your finances to assign money now and in the future. There are three utility domains where you can find life and money alignment and give your money assignments. What life stage you are in uniquely affects your preferences and purpose. We'll talk more about this in Chapters 4, 5, and 8, but here's the gist.

LIFE-CENTERED UTILITY

Life-centered Utility (LCU) facets are life-thriving areas that bring you fulfillment beyond measure, that bring meaning. The LCU domain carries a significant time cost and emotional intelligence understanding, requiring sufficient finances to purchase utility units.

For example, you can't measure the value of spending two weeks or a month with your family for an on-location vacation, or a staycation. The experience and time affluence are invaluable. Yet, the experience milestone requires the purchase of time and supporting elements. *Your point of life and financial situation determines your money allocations toward the facets unique to you.*

MONEY PSYCHOLOGY UTILITY

Money Psychology Utility (MPU) is facets that require investigation and investment to progress through and toward self-actualization. Wholeness of self is necessary to produce sufficient output, work from income to assets to wealth, invest in higher dimensions of self, and purchase intended levels of well-being.

For example, a mutually healthy spousal relationship objectively contributes to higher well-being and finances. Subjectively, relational utility is immeasurable, and its meaning is unbounded. There are stages in life where more attention (time) and investment (money) are needed to support your relationship. *Your point of life and financial situation determines your money allocations toward the facets unique to you.*

LIFESTYLE UTILITY

Lifestyle Utility (LSU) facets are tangible and intangible "wants," goods, and services with little external value except for mindful social capital, yet are high in internal value. Your lifestyle choices are less about external affirmation and more about internal actualization. Investing attention and support toward personal and quality-of-life preferences helps feed the "want" desires of self-actualization, serving as inspiration to remain connected to your wholeness journey without feelings of deprivation, judgment, or shame.

For example, purchasing luxury or custom clothing, subscribing to a country club membership, regular travel, buying art, or investing in an expensive hobby all have their social and individual interpretations of their value. Yep, you guessed it! *Your point of life and financial situation determines your money allocations toward the facets unique to you.*

LIFE STAGE VITALITY

Life Stage Vitality (LSV) considers physical and mental capability and lifestyle preferences within and across life stages, influencing trade-offs and preference order that affect choices and outcomes to maximize well-being now and in the future.

For example, take a Gen X coupled household in their 40s making high incomes. Yes, retirement is at the top of their mind, along with funding young adult children, potentially caring for elderly parents, and generational wealth or charitable legacy. But what about their current lifestyle? Do they forgo facets that are important to them now that they will not be able to do later or that may not hold the same importance to them in the next life? What if there's a travel excursion they can make now because they are more able-bodied?

What if having a newer car makes financial and necessary sense now and has a higher enjoyment factor than if they purchased the same car later in life? Like our personality domains tend to shift at older ages, so do our preferences and purpose choices across life stages. The point? Alas! *Your point of life and financial situation determines your money allocations toward the facets unique to you.*

LMB is about *balancing* the continuous interaction and investment in these domains and facets across and within themselves and across and within life stages. That's why the process of your finances doesn't stop with a plan. You are *planning.*

THE MUSIC OF YOUR MONEY

Living your *Wealth in the Key of Life* helps you find harmony with grace, grit, and gratitude. Financial compassion is your armored protection that shakes off self and societal shame and guilt, making you immune to parrots and the echo chambers of recycled thoughts. Your "Key of Life" is a system of integrated sounds that plays to the soul of your life and finances. Your soul is your total self, representing your unique essence, principles, and spirit. Finding harmony, keys, and melodies is essential to shaping your life's design and finances.

Quincy Jones is a global musical-producing genius. His career spans 70 years and touches every genre of music, from classical to jazz, rock, pop, big band, rap, country, and television and movie scores. There is no box for Mr. Jones. He is 1 of 18 EGOT (Emmy, Grammy, Oscar, Tony) Award winners and the producer of the greatest-selling record of all time, Michael Jackson's *Thriller*. He has worked with every musical artist, from Frank Sinatra to Duke Ellington. You know the *Austin Powers* theme song and "We Are the World"? Yes, those, too! He is the penultima of humanity. In his Netflix documentary *Quincy*, he said, "Music is so divine there are only 12 notes, everybody gets the same notes, we have to figure out how to make them ours through rhythm, harmony, and melody. Melody is King and Queen."[9]

Let's dive into musicology for a second. You'll see music as an accompanying theme throughout this book. Like money, music touches our soul with each song, carrying unique meaning for unique moments in our lives. Musical harmony is when two or more notes play or sing simultaneously, supporting and giving context to the melody. Harmony is made with instruments or voices. Melodies are musical notes played in specific sequences that form a unique unit. The melody has various pitches, tones, and durations and includes more than three notes.

The melody is the most iconic and memorable. You can hum or sing the melody of your favorite tunes immediately. For the most iconic, you can rip the melody off the top. Think of something simple like "Happy Birthday to You." You may think of "We Will Rock You" by Queen, "Billie Jean" by Michael Jackson, Nirvana's "Smells Like Teen Spirit," Whitney Houston's "I Will All Ways Love You," "C.R.E.A.M." by the WuTangClan, "Stayin' Alive" by the Bee Gees, or even Lady Gaga's "Poker Face."

L.S. Knost said, "Music speaks the language of the soul, penetrating into the past and resonating into the future, unearthing pain and tenderness and sorrow and joy, reminding us of our infinite fragility and extraordinary strength, reigniting our dreams and passions once again to remind us of who we are meant to be."

One writer wrote about Steve Wonder's all-time classic album *Songs in the Key of Life* – my personal life soundtrack. "*Songs in the Key of Life* lives up to its title, taking us on a journey through life. It is not a sequential path – the songs move somewhat randomly through birth and death, happiness and sadness, joy and pain, love and loss."[10] With alignment and aspiration, you can transform from pain to prosperity, roll and adapt through life's ebbs and flows, and achieve the life you envision.

SHUN SOCIAL MONEY STIGMAS

This book aims to push back on some oft-repeated personal finance platitudes that get people stuck in social shame, stigmas, or potential biases from financial experts and financial planning academia. That may sound weird coming from a so-called financial influencer, certified financial planning practitioner, financial planning academic, and champion of financial psychology. Much of the empirical or professional data are well-intentioned and mostly accurate in their findings. Furthermore, evidence-based information is sounder than misinformation. Data and theory help ground insight with the rigors of philosophy, science, and math.

The flaws in data collection, interpretation, and application infuse shame and judgment, parroting tropes and biases that make their way into commonly accepted principles that people *should* abide by. These misguidances deter or derail people from pursuing or persisting through the joys of finding life and financial harmony, their unique key of life: a path of contentment and fulfillment. At the same time, it pushes forward some notions, elevates others, and develops fresh perspectives. There must be space to remain objective about your journey's financial wellness and overall well-being while having a basis for understanding and incorporating your experiences and stories that brings unique logic to planning your finances.

It's time we changed our programs and perceptions with our lives and money. Money is a partner to your plan and purpose that highlights the Humanity of Money, presenting a holistic view of your money life. Throughout the book, you might read personal tidbits from my journey. In the therapy profession, it's called a Selective Share; I'm quickly sharing a story that I hope connects and communicates with a people-first feel to otherwise drab concepts that folks may not immediately connect with. The point is to share intentionally, always keeping your journey in mind. Please know this book is about you and your journey.

What I want for you from this book is to live the abundant and aspirational life you deserve with the compassion to strive and thrive in times of challenge to your champion life, being open to financial advice and education that advances your human condition and helps you better understand your LMB.

KEY TAKEAWAYS

- Life Money Balance *is* financial harmony through wealth-secured well-being.
- Money is a partner to your plan and purpose.
- Everyone has a unique story, and stories inform their numbers. When your life and money are aligned, your money has assignments.
- Our willingness to change and our decisions reflect our desire to achieve success in the way we define it.

CHAPTER ONE

ADMITTING WHERE YOU ARE

I often think of Michael Jackson's "Man in the Mirror," a song about honest self-reflection and willingness to change. The mirror can serve as a healthy audit or as an expensive tax. It starts with you; your journey is yours, and you must be willing to change. Change is hard because it requires courageous admission of where you are and a discovery of who you are.

That admission sparks the start! Sometimes, there are false starts because life doesn't function in a continuous, straight line – but with a genuine start, you have the readiness to get where you want to go with your life and finances. You'll notice that whichever point in your life's journey serves as your starting point to listen, research, take action, or fail to make a financial strategy, it always begins with questions of self: what, why, when, when, where, how?

The image in the mirror is healthy when your audit starts with a process of compassion that encourages reflection, generates motivation, and spurs action. The mirror can tax you for not acknowledging where you are or for avoiding action. Keeping your head in the sand leads to higher costs for wealth and well-being, and avoidance brings or compounds anxiety, giving rise to needless suffering.

People want more confidence in and clarity about their finances in order to control their life design. As we discussed in the introduction, they want to play their song in their key. A 2023 Gallup Poll asked Americans about their financial confidence, separating income brackets into lower, middle, and upper income.[11] Responders who reported their financial confidence using an index score of 100 plus, which is excellent or good, said they felt they were getting better at finance. Respondents who selected under 100 said their confidence in their finances was poor and was getting worse.

For upper-income Americans earning $100,000 or more, their financial confidence index was plus 28. For middle-income earners between $40,000 and $99,999, their score was negative 22; for lower-income Americans earning less than $40,000, their score was negative 43. In the same report, 62% of the aggregate Americans reported that they had enough to live comfortably, but if you peel back the onion, many still indicated that they had financial worries.

66% worry about having enough for retirement.

60% worry about high medical costs.

60% worry about inflation.

50% worry about maintaining a standard of living.

42% worry about not having enough to pay bills.

What do all these numbers mean? Generally, higher-income folks felt better about their current and future financial prospects. This makes sense because, with more funds, they can better fund their fundamental needs and aspirational wants, therefore funding more holistic well-being. Yet higher-income folks still worry about the domains and facets they value most. Unfortunately, asking the right questions to understand the root of that worry can be painful.

WRITE YOUR LETTER

One of the best things I ever did for myself was to write letters to myself during my admission stage. It took a couple of attempts for me to talk openly and honestly with myself without fear of judgment. In my letters, I expressed my greatest fears, shortcomings, and aspirations – but first, I had to admit what was troubling me, from my internal self of self-inflicted wounds, feelings, behaviors, and actions, and from both perceived and actual external forces. These letters are my love letters, and they are my letters of account. I find some ugliness in there, but there's also beauty.

Accompanying these letters are a couple of photos from these times that serve as mirrors for myself and reflections of what was happening in my life. I do not keep them as pictures of shame or judgment; however, you can see the feelings of shame, regret, and guilt in my eyes, the eyes of a person who wants to heal and pursue health across all life's domains, including finances.

To bring focus to my finances, I printed off three months' worth of bank and credit card statements during these turbulent times to see where my money was going. This discovery exercise helped reveal whether my money had any direction. Was my money telling a story of my life? Were my line items leading my life's course? If so, what was my life's intended direction, and was my money on the course? If not, why? How did I get here? What could I do to pivot? These are Honest Self-Audit questions.

I always keep these letters and photos in an envelope near my desk, within arm's reach. These letters serve as a reminder of what I've been through, an expression of gratitude for where I am, and a reminder of where I'm going. They are a reminder of what I don't want to do and of what I do want to do. Also in the envelope are pictures of my current self, my ideal self – reflections of a new energy. Positive affirmation statements and words of encouragement on the front help promote my flourishing. I share this with you because I ask the people I serve to trust the process. As a financial professional and educator who professes to advance the human condition through financial advice and education, I eat my own cooking, and I want the same tasty meal for you.

STORIES IN YOUR STATEMENTS: ELEMENTS OF YOUR LETTER

1. Identify the evidence of patterns in your life and money decisions.
2. Ask and answer challenging questions with brutal honesty.
3. Express compassion for your resilience through grace and gratitude.
4. Affirm your past and current self.
5. Define and encourage your future ideal self.

When you perform your audit, you will find stories in your bank and card statements. Because each person's story is unique, you'll find that your stories and statements could feel like *New York Times* bestsellers! The process of reflection is tough. However, challenging times are necessary to get to your future ideal self. Reframing these stories will keep you on track instead of avoiding the process. What's more, after addressing challenging times, there's a more positive outcome on the other side.

BETTER TO ADMIT THAN AVOID

Admitting where you are in your journey requires honest, bold, and courageous reflection and is the first step in the Honest Self-Audit (HSA). The

HSA is to *admit* where you are, *acknowledge* how you feel, and *act* on the change process. The first step is the hardest but serves to embrace the change, commitment, and consistency necessary to live and fund the life you envision without regret or explanation.

Understanding the *what* and *why* of being stuck begins with admitting you are, indeed, stuck! Admitting doesn't have to come from unpleasant feelings or experiences; the process can contain the positivity of wanting to move beyond where you currently stand. You can be stuck at any life stage, income, or wealth level. Being stuck is either not being where you want to be, being unsure of where you want to go, or having some understanding of where to go but lacking the knowledge of how to get there.

Admitting is the antidote to shame or judgment and opens the door to grace, gratitude, and grit, kicking off your aspirational journey. The opposite side of the spectrum is avoidance. Avoidant behavior is the biggest barrier to progress because it guaranTeas you remain stuck. Being stuck contributes to increased anxiety and saps the joy out of your journey. In financial psychology, money avoidance means avoiding your finances to avoid anxiety, worry, and stress. Avoidance does not alleviate emotional stress; it stacks on top of it.

AVOIDING MONEY IS AVOIDING YOUR LIFE

Cognitive avoidance is intentionally turning your mind away from thoughts or events that may bring you stress or anxiety and engaging in thoughts of "everything is going to be okay" or overly positive thoughts of positive outcomes while the current situation is not, in fact, going well.[12] Another avoidance tactic is **situational avoidance**, where people avoid activities, people, places, or things that trigger them.[12]

In financial psychology, there's a commonly referred to money mindset archetype called **money avoidance,** where people with this mindset believe that money is "bad," "wealthy people are greedy," or "they do not deserve money."[13] This could be a mix of social conditioning or social shame from individual cultural beliefs or experiences toward the rich. Some research suggests that people hold this mentality because of childhood flashpoints specific to an individual's upbringing. The *root* of **full-scope money avoidance** is not wanting to actively think about or address money issues that give you pause or trigger *you.* Using a full-scope approach to money avoidance, isolates cognitive and situational avoidance that helps focus on unique stressors, situations, experiences, and beliefs of the person, inclusive of child and adulthood, and not preconceived social constructs about money prosperity. It's the intentional act of dodging issues, dressing up untrue and undesirable outcomes of the present and future, and yielding money situations to external influences rather than addressing internal controls.

Avoiding your money is avoiding your life because it disconnects you from your stated self-aspirations, a separation of two selves, the ideal and the normal. Remember, the Humanistic Theory of Motivation suggests your ideal self is the person you envision and wish to be. Who you are now is your current self. To reach the pinnacle of self, your ideal and normal selves must work in harmony to shape your full self. Admitting where you are helps start that connecting process.

MONEY IS MORE THAN A TOOL – IT'S REPRESENTATIVE

One reason to begin an honest account of where your life and finances are is their relationship to your life and your identity. A positive correlation between two stocks means that two stock prices move in the same direction, and a negative correlation means that two stock prices tend to move in opposite directions.

Think of your life and money this way. During periods of alignment, your life and money move in unison during both ebbs and flows. During disjointed periods, the dysfunction rate in life increases, and your finances go down the drain. Knowing the relationship between life and money and exploring the nature of these stages helps explain why money is both dollars and cents and dollars and sense.

Let's break down what money is: Money is representative. It represents your identity, a sum of past and current experiences sewn into the fabric of your everyday existence. That's why money is so emotional – it truly is *personal* finance.

The Teas of Life (TOL) and The Teas of Money (TOM) help explain the Humanity of Money. The seasons of the TOL are *trial, triumph, transformation*, and *transition*. There are reasons for each season through which we learn and progress with resilience. Your TOLs and TOMs help connect, understand, align, and assign personal finances – finding your keys of life and giving your money soul.

The trial is a season of struggle where, through the fog, we seek a destination and answers. However, the discovery of self and support to bust through internal and external barriers can be challenging, yet there's a burning or hidden willingness for better well-being. Your triumphant milestones represent the resilience in making it through and to your place of understanding of where you want to be.

Celebrate and grab hold of your triumphant milestone moments to spark transformation. Transformation embraces change and encourages the mindset to sustain the change. Grace and secured self-worth give you internal permission to transition to your ideal self and not want to let go. Your TOLs help you find grace, grit, gratitude, and aspirations for your journey.

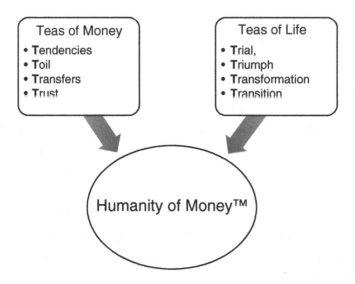

The Teas of Money are *tendency*, *toil*, *transfers*, and *trust*. They represent the human capital and emotional intelligence we place in the money we produce.

Your tendencies represent your natural or patterned habits, behaviors, thoughts, and choices. Your preferences and programs are embedded in your tendencies, and discovery helps you define values and areas that require addressing. Toil is the "blood, sweat, and tears" factor. It represents the time, talent, sacrifice, and commitment required – work – to produce financial resources – money.

Transfers are intentional financial and emotional investments we make to our loved ones and selves to secure our desired well-being. Transfers are willing giving of self and sources. Trust is a virtue that finds us at our most vulnerable and one of our most valuable assets to be earned and extended. Think of how much trust goes into your finances with yourself, your spouse, friends, family, advisors, investments, charitable giving, and where you choose to spend your money. Your TOMs help you find what you value most and give alignment to your money.

"Money is a tool" is a common saying in personal finance. I get it: by definition, a tool is used to carry out a function. By interpretation, money helps us carry out our lives. Taking this one step further to make life's journey meaningful, we should place money in its proper place as the tool, not the goal. However, this approach flagrantly understates money's role in life and the essence of finances in our existence and experience. Money represents our being, helping describe why money is deeply personal and emotional.

When critics or commenters say money is not a goal, they are grappling with the context of contentment and the push and pull between "more" and "enough." If your quest for more money is the *only* goal, then yes, your thirst will never be quenched. The maladjusted thought of your self-worth being your net worth is a damaging money belief, leaving no room for personal fulfillment. That goal of "if I had more money, then I could do, have, or be more" is a greyhound chasing a mechanical rabbit at a dog race – an endless chase.

The goal of "enough" resides alongside fulfillment, landing at contentment. Because finding what brings us fulfillment and what amount fills "enough" buckets coexist, it's fair that both life *and* money are the goals. What we invest in both buckets is an investment in our human condition. Wanting more money to fulfill your "enough" bucket is okay. The bold and courageous study of your "enough" helps you understand your "more than enough."

When money takes up more account space, it takes up less mind space. Unlocking your "more than enough" guides your "how-much-more" journey – it gives you confidence and clarity to race at your pace. Admitting where we are requires a moment of honesty; you need to play the tape and hear the music.

In economics, money is a medium of exchange that uses currency to facilitate the purchase of a good or service. The human version of the medium of exchange is a person's wholeness produces money that facilitates the purchase of fulfillment. Life *and* money are the goals. Understanding your goal journey is the gold.

STAGES OF CHANGE

The Stages of Change Model was released to the world in the early 1980s.[14,15,16,17] The change model was developed by studying the willingness of cigarette smokers to engage in the behavior change necessary to quit smoking. The study's outcome was that people progress through five stages of change when trying to modify their behavior toward an aspiration of their choosing. The model outlines the steps toward progress and potential barriers where people get stuck when engaging in change behavior and sustaining and maintaining the behavior that is best for their well-being. The stages of change are about their readiness and willingness to change.

There's a saying: "If you stay ready, you never have to get ready." Well, that's after you have learned how to *be* ready. The six stages are precontemplation (not ready), contemplation (getting ready to act), preparation (ready to take action), action, maintenance, and termination. Translating the stages to feelings and time frames, "not ready" lasts six months, "getting ready to act" happens within six months, "ready to take action" occurs within 30 days, and "taking action" lasts 30 days. After that, your action has a change effect lasting more than six months (maintenance), and then lasting change confidence takes hold with no relapse (termination). Your journey moves you from "intent to change" to behavior change through internal accountability.

What does this have to do with financial planning? Like the stages of change, financial planning is person-centered, uniquely personal, and requires a process. By the CFP Board standard, financial planning is the collaborative process that helps maximize a person's potential for meeting life goals through financial advice that integrates relevant elements of a person's personal and financial circumstances. Furthermore, certified financial planner professionals and financial advisors holding the CFP designation are required to put the best interests of the client first at all times, which is called being a fiduciary.

The parallels of the Change Model, the Teas of Life, the Honest Self Audit, and the personal finance process are apparent – blending self, change, solutions, control, psychology, well-being, finances, and the process of planning your life and finances.[18,19] Admitting where you are requires compassion and courage to perform an open and honest self-audit that helps discover the *why* behind your life and finances and where any disconnect is. My mother once told me the same thing: You celebrate champion moments in your life and don't regret the challenging moments; there are reasons for seasons. She is right.

REFLECT TO RESTART

Reflection helps grasp the self-awareness you need to begin the change process – admitting being stuck through choice, practices, and aspirational disconnects. Reality can be scary, and you may possess some shame. Living in unknowns can spark a willingness to experience better knowns. Internal shame, different from external shaming from others, can spark a willingness to reverse course and not lose an opportunity. Recognizing reality can be awakening and freeing, too, finding inspiration to go after your true aspiration boldly. The courage of self-awareness and vulnerability opens the door to transformation.

Admitting where you are is the opening chord to your song, and the mirror is your key. Being real about your life and finances will help encourage you to embrace the change you need to align your dollars with your purpose on a journey from trial through triumph, transformation, and transition.

WHAT DOES ADMITTING HAVE TO DO WITH THE MONEY?

Let's consider Aiden, age 40, who achieved early career success earning a high six-figure income, including a bonus. During his career tenure, he did not initiate any alignment between his life and finances. He instead adopted an approach of immensely enjoying his new lifestyle and delayed addressing near- and long-term finances.

With a new milestone event and increased finances, Aiden did not pause to audit his life stage to help him identify his ideal self. He did not begin funding his emergency fund, nor did he begin saving and investing for his future self. Then, he experienced a shocking job loss that shook him to his core, sending him into a spiral. Unfortunately, no funds were set aside for unexpected events, and the shame and guilt of the experience opened past and current emotional wounds. Not having money to absorb the shock and provide time for adjustment exacerbated his spiral, fueling a few directionless years where his finances were feeding unresolved emotions before, during, and after the career success.

Eventually hitting rock bottom, Aiden took a moment to audit what he didn't want to do anymore and then admitted that his life and finances were not aligned with where he aspired to be. The admission was overdue because that delay extended a lengthy period of directionless living and emotional suffering. Yet, it was on time because rock bottom was the first step in finding his keys to life and opening the door to the next steps.

There may be many factors that caused Aiden's life and money to be disjointed during this life stage. Money motivation does not always have to be spurred by trial; we'll have more upbeat stories about money throughout this book. Consider what taking an initial pause after career success could have yielded for Aiden, both financially and in terms of well-being. Could alignment have given him a new life direction or provided time to fund a well-being healing and finance-building process? With aligned life and money, could there have been an emergency fund to provide time to heal and stem the spiral or avoid the spiral altogether?

Stories abound, like the fictional account of Aiden. Your story may not be this drastic, but the most important thing to remember about the admitting stage is that it's unique to every person. Every person will have a different life and money turning point, and there's no shame or judgment in that. The admission stage doesn't have to directly follow a major trial period or event; it could simply be an admission of readiness for a life stage transition. Whichever point you begin, admitting is the toughest step, partly influenced by our natural inclination to cognitive dissonance.

COGNITIVE DISSONANCE

A mental validation where a person holds two conflicting versions of their beliefs, attitudes, and values and engaging in actions that help minimize the feeling of those inconsistencies.

The feelings associated with cognitive dissonance are shame, guilt, regret, and embarrassment, all of which are versions of inner turmoil and conflict. By holding onto a fundamental value system, part of your human dimension, something that may have been instilled in you or that you want to live your life by, you act in a way that does not align with your personal statement of life. Cognitive dissonance simply doesn't feel good when it comes to your well-being, and it can be costly to your finances.

There are many examples of life and finance misalignments that folks continue to engage in because they temporarily feel good, but that prolong a serious issue that will continue to deepen without proper address. An example could be not pursuing the career or life course that you want, which could lead to states of depression or a lack of fulfillment. On the financial side, it could mean impulse spending, not saving for future retirement, racking up debt, keeping up with the Joneses, FOMO (fear of missing out), limiting beliefs or scarcity mentalities, financial traumas, couples conflict, or lack of family boundaries.

Moving beyond these cognitive dissonances requires compassion and grace, first from the inner self and second from a support group. The next step requires courage and vulnerability to openly and honestly admit that there is a problem at hand that requires immediate attention, a willingness to change, space to process, and a framework that encourages action.

The first step, admitting, has everything to do with money and, most importantly, your life outcomes. Financial advisors have a famous line: They cannot guarantee investment returns. What I can guarantee is that for some of you reading this book, doing nothing – making no change – guaranTeas that the results won't change. But you can be encouraged: though there may be pain in admitting where you are, it is the first step toward joy and a promise for what is to come!

KEY TAKEAWAYS

- Reflection helps grasp the self-awareness you need to begin the change process – admitting.
- You must be willing to change. Change is hard because it requires courageous admission of where you are and a discovery of who you are.
- Like the stages of change, financial planning is person centered, uniquely personal, and requires a process.
- Being real about your life and finances will help encourage you to embrace the change you need to align your dollars with your purpose on a journey from trial through triumph, transformation, and transition.

Journal to Find Your Financial Harmony

Feelings + Finances helps your Finances Flourish. Take time to reflect on the takeaways in this chapter. Enjoy your time and journal only what connects with you most. Any findings during your journaling discovery will help you activate the Five-Point Life Planning Process.

- What life and money themes in this chapter speak specifically to your journey?
- Can you identify opportunities in your feelings and finances to align your life and money aspirations better, giving your money assignments to achieve the life you want?
- Were there any messages in the chapter that helped you:
  - Shake social money stigmas.
  - Release or address money anxiety, judgment, or shame.
  - Move toward better security and understanding of your finances.
  - Find more contentment or fulfillment or want to find some.
  - Discover or improve your relationship with money.
- Scan the Life Money Balance® Wheel, the Six-A-Alignment System™, and the Humanity of Money™. Did content in the chapter help you see yourself in a life stage, season, preference, domain, aspiration, money goal, or mindset?

Journaling Page

_____

_____

_____

_____

_____

_____

_____

_____

_____

_____

_____

_____

_____

_____

_____

_____

CHAPTER TWO

ACKNOWLEDGING HOW YOU FEEL ABOUT MONEY

You may be familiar with the concept of the green room, where performers go to mentally prepare themselves or reflect on the events before or after the show. Why it's called the green room is a mystery.[20,21] Historical uses are sporadic, but the modern-day commonly accepted use is for a place to relax, decompress, collect your thoughts, and take inventory of emotions before performing the show. The green room is also a place to hype yourself, to celebrate the joy of the moment and use the energy to propel the next action.

However, the room may be full of noise and distractions, too! Both internal and external noise are barriers to the preparation process. Internal noises are limiting beliefs in your ability or worthiness to live an abundant life as you define it. External noises are beyond our control because they reflect the thoughts, values, and actions of others. There is one way to control external noises: block them.

ACKNOWLEDGING HELPS CLEAR YOUR SOUL TO ACT

Acknowledging how you feel about money helps you gather yourself before you act in your journey, both internally and externally. Internal processing is a reflective self-audit that opens the door to accountability. Your audit reveals shortcomings in the habits, decisions, and choices you make when pursuing the life you want. Processing also offers space for grace, allowing you to forgive yourself for mistakes or shortcomings. Grace helps you break free of guilt and shame so you can transform failure moments into lessons. You then use your lessons as inspiring building blocks to motivate knowing *and* doing better. Additionally, the process addresses your relationship with money, helping you shake off social stigmas. Having the space to reset your money relationships and principles allows you to match your finances with your most important aspirations and values, protecting you from external judgment or shame.

During this phase, you find the space to give yourself grace and permission to forgive yourself for your shortcomings. One important theme you'll hear throughout this book is that relationships with money – past, present, and future – don't always have to come from a place of pain. Shortcomings can be challenging self-inflicted events, regular life occurrences, or perhaps life. It's okay. Still, you feel that you are not as far along as you want to be, you lack joy or fulfillment, and you aspire to create your life design. Regardless of the origin, acknowledging how you feel helps clear the barriers to progress and readies the self for confident action.

Clearing roadblocks allows you to drive a clear path in the direction you want to go. There's nothing like breaking out of a traffic jam. One yearly forecast of the average time commuters spend in traffic is between 100 and 150 hours annually.[22] Being from Houston, one of the traffic capitals of the world, I've learned you can handle traffic in two ways: you can have the mindset of inching forward and pushing through, knowing that ultimately there will be a breakthrough to your destination, or you can possess a mindset of being stuck, feeling there's no end and no possibility of breaking through the traffic.

What you do in traffic helps you work your way through the time. For example, listening to your favorite podcast, windshield time talking with loved ones, listening to classical music, or sitting in the melancholy of silence helps navigate the experience with connection and reflection. Conversely, not processing the experience with the noise of agitating music, combative news, or loud silence will certainly contribute to feeling stuck every day and to days of unfulfillment. You will feel like you are in the same scene over and over again, as in *Groundhog Day*.

COURAGE OPENS CLOSED DOORS

Addressing your feelings with courage helps clear your energy and remove regret, shame, guilt, and comparisons. With more self-space, you can swap out doubt with a firm belief in the possibility of positive outcomes and your worthiness of abundance, moving you to act on your wealth and well-being aspirations. Your progression through this stage may take three minutes, three days, three weeks, three months, or three years. The progression timeline is a personal process, powered by a distinct motivation motor to stop what's not working for you and start what will work for you. Only you can understand the power of desire that activates your pursuit. The idea here is to keep moving. Another message I often return to from Dr. King's "Blueprint" speech was resilience. He said, "If you can't fly, then run. If you can't run, then walk. If you can't walk, then crawl, but whatever you do, you have to keep moving."

Because money is woven through every fabric of our lives, this stage requires that we audit every event where we think we could or can do better. The key is digging around to get to the root, pulling the weed, and planting a seed for new growth – which is the future. Prepping your mind and spirit for the future is as important as exploring the past and present factors. Breaking through creates hope, action, and aspiration; acknowledging your money journey opens the door to hope.

JOURNAL YOUR JOURNEY

I realize we are in the digital age where many solutions are provided through tech, but as a Gen Xer, I know that sometimes the old school is the best. Acknowledgment can start with a pen and paper. Writing things down through journaling is a science-backed strategy to help unpack your emotions, gain perspective, and express yourself in private without shame or judgment.[23] You may be familiar with the healing and restorative feeling of writing in a journal. *Writing* works because it requires time, mindfulness, and intent. The connection of pen to paper helps compassionately connect your inner and ideal self by moving what's in your soul from conceptual to concrete, providing more clarity in your pursuit of understanding or expressing.

Journaling is the tool, and what you express through it is your story, narrated by you. Promoted by leading psychologists in the 1990s, narrative therapy allows you to tell your story, review how you see your life events, pull out narrow and negative memories from those events, and boost those events in a more positive light.[24] Affirming how you feel about life and money by channeling your feelings is essential; grace and forgiveness happen when you reshape how you identify with those events and how you use those memories to do things differently going forward. You are preparing yourself for your forward journey, finding harmony through intentional acknowledgment. Start with these harmony questions that help discover your past:

LMB QUESTIONS TO FIND YOUR HARMONY

1. In the past 12 months, what life and money event have you experienced that you would do differently?

2. Describe your emotions about the event.

3. What lessons or insights did you learn?

4. Now that you feel better informed emotionally and insightfully, what would you have done differently to promote your desired outcome?

5. Describe how you feel about your updated outcome.

These questions are a discovery tree that examines a recent past event through a before-and-after lens that identifies and reimagines the event to unlock emotions and outcomes. The pathway helps locate and unpack a recent undesired outcome with an informed desirable outcome by comparing the emotional and financial experiences of each. With a better understanding of the emotion attached to wanted and unwanted outcomes, with the *wanted* outcome having the better feeling and result, you may become more open to an objective information and discovery process (financial planning and financial therapy) with a better chance of achieving your goal. A psychological study from 2005 suggests that coupling writing about the event with expressing your emotions about the event leads to more optimal well-being outcomes than just writing about events or emotions singularly.[23] By tying your emotions to the event, not only are you processing how you feel or felt during flashpoint events, but you are also discovering how your "don't want to do's" feel compared to your ideal self – your "do want to do's." Establishing an emotion and event baseline helps align your life and money.

IMAGINE THE POWER OF JOURNALING

Have you ever spent the time writing a letter to a loved one or a friend, either longhand or by computer? When you are writing a letter to someone else, you are taking a pause out of life, thinking, reflecting, and pouring emotion into what you want to say to the person who is going to read it. When you are writing the letter, you are having the conversation in your heart, mind, and spirit. You can visualize the letter as though you are having a conversation with that person right at that moment.

As you envision the conversation, the energy is transferring from your soul through your hands to your pen or keyboard. Some of your energy, a piece of your soul, transports to the receiver in ways that a text, emoji, or other shortform communication doesn't do as well. Writing to yourself works in the same way; in solitude, you are connecting with yourself in a way that conveys compassion and sets the stage for the healing process.

Retelling your story through journaling or letter writing helps you see your life and money events in a different light. At first, your flashpoint events might seem like epic failures, leaving feelings of shame, guilt, regret, and perhaps external blame. Those feelings are valid, and your accountability is commendable. However, labeling yourself as a forever maladaptive person will only keep you stuck.

Acknowledging your resilience reshapes those events as contributors to your current enlightenment; it energizes you for change and commitment to the path. There are reasons for regressive and progressive seasons that help us admit where we are, acknowledge how we feel about it, and act toward our transformative stage. Previously neglected opportunities to maximize oneself and live in a healthy mental and financial well-being state can feel gloomy, casting a shadow on your future perceptions and muting the music of your aspiration. Acknowledging how you feel transforms those potential pain points of the past into gratitude and fuels you for future action.

What Does Acknowledging Have to Do with the Money?

Meg is stuck in both her finances and well-being. She is doing well professionally but knows she could be doing better. She makes a decent salary but is not saving enough. She spends every check to the bone, sometimes overspending to the point where she has to borrow from family members. Her net worth is negative, so none of her money is going toward self-investment, current well-being, or her ideal self or future self. Her retirement savings rate for the future is nonexistent, and most significantly, Meg has not identified her purpose – what brings her meaning and fulfillment. Meg's money is being thrown into a black hole; with her never-ending spending, her money is leading her life.

Meg makes $200,000 a year; 20% of that is $40,000 in savings, and the rest goes toward taxes and discretionary spending. Time is of the essence when saving for your future. Let's say while Meg is searching for her purpose through spending, she forgoes five years of $40,000 in savings per year across 20 years. If she invested in the market and realized an inflation-adjusted return of 6% over that time, her portfolio at the end of 20 years, *absent those five years*, would have a balance of $986,901. If Meg had saved $40,000 *throughout the entire 20 years* of her portfolio, its balance would be $1,471,424 – a difference of approximately $484,523.

Life is not linear, and there is no shame or judgment in how life should go; this entire book is about having a better understanding about the inner self and how life aligns with money and how that alignment can give your money assignments. What this mini–case study demonstrates is that the Humanity of Money influences well-being and wealth – the latter can be measured in dollars. In Meg's case, it was almost half a million dollars!

Meg's main Teas of Life is trial. She courageously raises her hand to voice her suffering from a lack of direction and purpose. She's ready to begin the admitting and acknowledgment stages and preparing for action toward transformation. With room to admit and acknowledge, there's also room to affirm triumph. In Meg's story, she successfully secures a high income through her profession, which coincides with her toil inside the Teas of Money. Within the TOMs, she's ready to transfer investments to achieve a better version of her ideal and future self – her version, no one else's. Also, by raising her hand, she's willing to trust her community circle and advice professionals and let the process steer her toward her version of success.

I get asked all the time, "What does all of this have to do with the money?" In other words, when are you, the financial advisor, going to show us what to do with our money? Unfortunately, you cannot get to the strategies of IRAs, 401k investment planning, estate planning, employee benefits, insurance planning, tax planning, or business owner planning without discussing the most essential domain of financial planning, which is the psychology of financial planning – the Humanity of Money.

What are the keys of your life? In this case, Meg must acknowledge her feelings about her spending and the cost of the discovery. There is redemptive value in auditing your feelings, not living with the regret of losing a quarter million to a million dollars of time, opportunity, and money. There's also possible shame or guilt that must be processed while acknowledging this cost, which takes courage and vulnerability. The positive of this process is that allowing oneself to go through an honest self-audit of acknowledgment of emotion clears the way to the next stage, moving toward clear-mindedness and full energy. Then, you can take action toward your life and money aspirations and commit to the strategies that will bring Harmony to both.

KEY TAKEAWAYS

- Internal processing (acknowledging) is a reflective self-audit that opens the door to accountability. Your audit reveals shortcomings in your habits, decisions, and choices when pursuing the life you want.
- Retelling your story through journaling or letter writing helps you see your life and money events in a different light and shake shame, guilt, and regret.
- In tying your emotions to the event, not only are you processing how you feel or felt during flashpoint events, but you are also discovering how your "don't want to do's" feel compared to your ideal self – your "do want to do's."
- Delays in addressing your self-care costs dollars in your wealth-building journey.

Journal to Find Your Financial Harmony

Feelings + Finances helps your Finances Flourish. Take time to reflect on the takeaways in this chapter. Enjoy your time and journal only what connects with you most. Any findings during your journaling discovery will help you activate the Five-Point Life Planning Process.

- What life and money themes in this chapter speak specifically to your journey?
- Can you identify opportunities in your feelings and finances to align your life and money aspirations better, giving your money assignments to achieve the life you want?
- Were there any messages in the chapter that helped you:
  - Shake social money stigmas.
  - Release or address money anxiety, judgment, or shame.
  - Move toward better security and understanding of your finances.
  - Find more contentment or fulfillment or want to find some.
  - Discover or improve your relationship with money.
- Scan the Life Money Balance® Wheel, the Six-A-Alignment System™, and the Humanity of Money™. Did content in the chapter help you see yourself in a life stage, season, preference, domain, aspiration, money goal, or mindset?

Journaling Page

_____

_____

_____

_____

_____

_____

_____

_____

_____

_____

_____

_____

_____

_____

_____

_____

_____

_____

_____

_____

_____

_____

_____

_____

_____

_____

_____

_____

_____

_____

_____

_____

_____

_____

_____

CHAPTER THREE

SURVIVING FINANCIAL TRIALS WITH RESILIENCE

T he are four seasons, and all four are necessary to nourish life. In different geographies, seasons may last longer, be harsher, or seem more majestic than in others. I'm from Houston, Texas, where summer temperatures reach 100-plus degrees, and when you factor in the humidity it is brutal. I thought Houston was the most humid place in the United States, but it turns out that Texas has 3 of the top 10 hottest cities in the United States and Houston comes in at eighth.[25] Now, that's not saying much because 64% humidity is considered average and levels above that become downright uncomfortable; the top 10 hottest cities range from 89 to 90 average annual humidity.[26] In addition to humidity, Houston has drenching and devasting thunderstorms throughout the year and is exposed to floods and hurricanes.

Compare Houston to more northern areas like Green Bay, Wisconsin, where there is average to below-average humidity, but you can exchange extreme heat for brutally cold winters. Green Bay is one of the 14 coldest cities in the United States; Wisconsin is the tenth coldest State.[27] In a Wisconsin winter, windchills can get to −20 and −30°, with temperatures in the negative teens, and snow can stretch across 6 months. One person being from one city and looking at the other can say each has uncomfortable seasons, with different kinds of seasons being worse than the others. The seasons are objectively necessary for these respective places and subjectively relative to the people within those cities. Seasons have their unique effect on their region and residents.

Human seasons come upon people at unpredictable times but happen at intentional times to the intended person and with the intended purpose. Some seasons have their times of paradise and others their times of turmoil. In each case, when the weather is at its most challenging, to persevere through requires your grit, resilience, adjustment, reflection – and even sometimes regret (as in "Why in the hell did I stay here so long?"). This too reflects our life and money. As my mother once said to me, "Forgive yourself and let go of guilt and regret. Your life has seasons and there are reasons for seasons; those seasons are the reason why you are here and why you are who you are in this moment."

WORKING THROUGH MONEY TRAUMA

Money is sometimes considered taboo because of money trauma, either from internal or external environments. Exploring money relationships and money lessons for financial health doesn't always have to come from challenging or uncomfortable times; in Chapter 7 we will discuss the ways that money memories can be from pleasant times that we can champion. For now, our purpose is turning from trial that grips you to grace, which you can grow from.

Sometimes people choose to avoid money to avoid addressing or reliving past or current relationships with money. We've discussed how money is representative and part of our existence. Acknowledging your feelings about your seasons in your life is one thing; recognizing the meaning of those feelings is another.

Understanding the root of your life events, whether positive or challenging, and your prevailing self-defeating thoughts and interpretations of events, whether influenced by external causes or self-inflicted, helps you uncover the meaning of your discourse. Understanding meaning can help sort wrapped thoughts, decisions, and behaviors borne from the event, unlocking new meaning for your charted course.

UNCERTAINTY IS CERTAIN

The theory that supports cognitive behavioral therapy suggests that the happenings of our lives influence our thoughts, feelings, and behaviors, and that this connected system of facets shapes our current behavior.[28] With life and money, uncertainty is certain. While there's no guarantee of investment returns, you are guaranteed that life will ebb and flow through highs and lows. The good news is that you do not have to wait for the other shoe to drop, but being better prepared helps soften the effects of those ebbs and flows.

When life's challenges present themselves, we must embrace a "roll and adapt" mentality that demonstrates perseverance and adjustment. There are other times when the internal life void is too big where the lack of meaning persists, disconnecting your purpose from your money. How do you investigate these periods of trial through a financial harmony perspective? Recall that there are stories in your statements. You can discover the fissures of life because your money follows your meaning, and your financial statements don't lie.

YOUR FINANCIAL STATEMENTS MATTER

Often, while helping clients through the financial planning process and after asking for financial statements, there are documents I receive quickly and others I must ask for more than once. People are willing to provide their summary bank or credit card statements, and the first couple pages of the statement provide the total inflows minus the outflows for the period, monthly or quarterly, at the aggregate level but not the detailed level. The client will say, "I sent you that," or "I uploaded that document already." I respond, "Yes, I appreciate that. However, can you please send the detailed line-item statement accompanying the summary statement?"

Turning over intimate details of your money flows gives objective insights into your money life. Matching your statement of financial purpose with your detailed financial statements quickly reveals life and money misalignments. Identifying these gaps is a vulnerable ordeal. The philosophy of LMB, of letting your life lead your money, could not be more applicable than in an alignment audit. Your financial statements will help you uncover your season of fog and help you ask, what does or did this season mean? You may not even know that you are in trial season until you review and reflect on your statements. Your statements could be your only source of truth.

When you tap into your story, you tap into your money; it helps you understand these things more deeply. When folks are at the mercy of the fog, they can find their emotions, energy, and money aimlessly funding the habits of the fog. Life and money aspirations moving in opposite directions, at odds with one another, contributes to increased opportunity costs.

These forgone opportunities to maximize oneself and live in a healthy state of mental and financial well-being feel gloomy and cast a shadow on future perceptions. Failures and fallbacks will require you to roll and adapt, calling on all of your resilience energy.

By allowing your period or trial to extend, distortions of thought and behavior manifest, and guilt will gut the aspirations you have inside. Chances are you see the events of fog darker than the actual events and are harder on yourself than need be.

By courageously asking the questions of investigation, you gain more clarity, and you can begin investing your dollars in the healing you need to unlock meaning in times past. You begin to create the life you want, matching the stories of your financial statements with your statement of financial purpose. In these moments, you don't want to be low on resilience energy.

Resilience energy can help propel your breakout moment. Remain steadfast in the award and reward part of your journey. The reward is the everyday practice of the pursuit of small wins that may not feel like big wins, but they are. You get by gaining every day. Living the lifestyle of leaning into your aspirations is rewarding. Achieving the goals in your aspirations is the award. In life and money, there are more reward days than award days. Without resilience, you miss out on the rewarding joy and the awards of fulfillment.

WHAT DOES RESILIENCE HAVE TO DO WITH THE MONEY?

"It's never too late" is cliche but also very applicable to your life and your money. In planning for retirement, I always ask people, "Do you like ketchup?" Many folks in their money journey – even those with higher incomes – don't feel confident in their retirement accounts and wealth prospects. They feel behind relative to where they perceive they should be or compared to where others are. While I don't like to use the word *should* because most folks don't feel confident in their money journeys, I jokingly say, "They should like ketchup!" or, if you missed the pun, "catch up!" *It's never too late.*

The great actor Samuel L Jackson has courageously shared his story about his drug and alcohol abuse for a couple of decades, from childhood through his late 30s. He was able to become an accomplished and recognized actor but admits he left a lot on the table during those years, recognizing that there was misalignment in his meaning and purpose and that he was tired. He began getting sober in 1991 around the age of 40 and with only weeks of sobriety landed a role in Spike Lee's *Jungle Fever*, which is recognized as his breakout role – where, ironically, he played a struggling crackhead. Samuel Jackson today is one of the highest-grossing and highest-paid actors of all time. *It's never too late.* Once he found out his "why" in his story and meaning and purpose in life, his life and money began to flourish. He naturally was able to catch up. You can too!

LMB LESSON: LIFE AND MONEY ALIGNMENT GIVES MONEY ASSIGNMENTS

1. Increase retirement savings rates beyond 15% during high-income years. Try to approach 20–25%, perhaps 30%. The key is matching your savings rate to your retirement date.

2. In tax-deferred retirement accounts after age 50, there are additional catchup amounts that increase every year that are in addition to contribution amounts that allow folks who feel behind to contribute more during the high-income years to put away more for retirement.

For example, for the year 2024, the pretax contribution limit for employer-sponsored plans like 401Ks is $23,000. The allowed catch-up amount is $7,500, which is in addition to the original, bringing the total to $30,500.

In the case of Meg from Chapter 2, what were her inner detours? Finding out your "why" is worth more in the long run than keeping those feelings inside. First, it just doesn't feel good. Second, the longer the delay of your investigation, the longer the money goes into a black hole.

Discovering the "why" is essential to LMB. Resilience takes tapping into life and money alignment and giving money assignments. Meg can now take dollars that were going into the abyss and, even though they may not be going into emergency funds or investment accounts, put them into her investment of self. A healthy self can produce both income and well-being that will compound over time.

KEY TAKEAWAYS

- Human seasons come upon people at unpredictable times but happen at intentional times to the intended person and with the intended purpose.
- Forgive yourself and let go of guilt and regret. Your life has seasons, and there are reasons for seasons; those seasons are the reason why you are here and why you are who you are in this moment.
- Your financial statements will help you uncover your season of fog and help you ask, what does or did this season mean?
- When you tap into your story, you tap into your money.

Journal to Find Your Financial Harmony

Feelings + Finances helps your Finances Flourish. Take time to reflect on the takeaways in this chapter. Enjoy your time and journal only what connects with you most. Any findings during your journaling discovery will help you activate the Five-Point Life Planning Process.

- What life and money themes in this chapter speak specifically to your journey?
- Can you identify opportunities in your feelings and finances to align your life and money aspirations better, giving your money assignments to achieve the life you want?
- Were there any messages in the chapter that helped you:
  - Shake social money stigmas.
  - Release or address money anxiety, judgment, or shame.
  - Move toward better security and understanding of your finances.
  - Find more contentment or fulfillment or want to find some.
  - Discover or improve your relationship with money.
- Scan the Life Money Balance® Wheel, the Six-A-Alignment System™, and the Humanity of Money™. Did content in the chapter help you see yourself in a life stage, season, preference, domain, aspiration, money goal, or mindset?

Journaling Page

_____

_____

_____

_____

_____

_____

_____

_____

_____

_____

_____

_____

_____

_____

_____

_____

_____

_____

CHAPTER FOUR

TAKING MINDFUL ACTION

OPTIMISM

There are many examples of signals that snap us into action, and when we receive them, there's no better time to be intentional about the change you want for the present and future. Action relieves anxiety and uncertainty and promotes confidence in living the life you envision.

I was watching a television series once, and the question was asked, "Why do you use cliches so much?" The answer was "because they work." Speaking of TV, it is time to make your movie, your "lights, camera, action!" What contraption snaps us to attention in movies? The clapperboard. The clap was pioneered by F.W. Tring and Leon M. Leon, who developed the clapboard and later added the slate board.

The clapboard is used for every film taken during the filmmaking process, helping organize the scene shooting and the postproduction process.[29] The clapper marks scenes with essential information such as the date, title, the director's name, and information about the scene. Modern clapboards are scribed with chalk or dry-erase makers, updating the information for each scene, and the famous *clack* sound is the signal for upcoming action. Then the magic happens.

ACTIVATE YOUR LIFE'S COURSE

Gathering yourself, collecting information, experiencing your call to action, and then the stage-maker – these all perfectly describe the action moment of your life stage. There are scenes that later, in the metaphorical post-production life stages, you will reflect upon and say, "That was the moment that changed my life." Deciding to act is a milestone moment. You'll recall the moments with cliches like "I can remember it like it was yesterday" and "I remember what clicked for me!" The readiness is freeing, the beginning of charting the course to the life you envision with the freedom to live now and in the future.

This life and money stage requires mindfulness and a solutions focus, helping you move from stagnation to striving. Though it was key earlier, overfocusing on acknowledging past emotions and events now doesn't allow for progress. The future gives us hope, hope inspires aspiration, and aspirations ignite action.

BRING MINDFULNESS TO YOUR LIFE MONEY BALANCE

Mindfulness prompts folks to be more aware, to practice acceptance, and to focus on the present instead of the past.[30] Mindfulness is an essential next step after the acknowledgment stage, which placed your audit attention on the past. While you are in the reflection mode from acknowledging, reflection influences what you want now for your holistic self, contributing to how you go about making conscious decisions that feed and fund both current and future fulfillment.

The most important part of mindfulness, while you are being aware, is promoting inner peace. You are now in a clear state for healthy analysis and a better state for action. Popular mindful practices to bring you into the present are environment regulations such as intentional breath patterns, feng shui surroundings, journaling, pauses for reflection, and physical activity such as yoga.

One academic study suggests that mindfulness brings people too much into the present, placing more emphasis on the current self and discounting the future self by transferring money away from long-term investments toward the most present life, engaging only in the near-term.[31] Many leading mindfulness experts appreciate the study of mindfulness and money but push back on using only the "mindful" exercise called "the five-minute meditation recording" to represent the practice of mindfulness.[32] One such person is my friend and renowned financial psychology and financial therapy pioneer Saundra Davis, who says that how you practice mindfulness matters to the effectiveness of mindfulness.

Mindfulness takes more than five minutes, and while the "meditation recording" is used in the study to simulate mindfulness, the time, depth, and mindfulness practice can affect the state of presence brought forth and thus affect outcomes and interpretations. Furthermore, *shouldn't* you become more present and allocate dollars to your current self? Better health contributes to better wealth. A healthier self could increase your *near-term* well-being, building a better self for clarity and stamina for commitment and stick-to-itiveness of *long-term* goals. Lastly, bringing about mindfulness with dedicated time helps spark awareness, allowing you to be in a state of presence that opens the heart and mind to connect with the life and finances you envision.

LMB REFRAMES REGRET

The LMB philosophy emphasizes the integration of facets that link your current self to your future self, striking a respectful balance between life stages to unite your selves as one. We often hear what people do and don't say on their deathbeds, with many pointing out that folks don't talk about money on their deathbeds and that money is not in the top mentions of regret. The popular *Top Five Regrets of the Dying: A Life Transformed by the Dearly Departing* by Bronnie Ware is about an end-of-life care specialist who writes about caring for people on their last day; she tells stories of people's last thoughts and shares their fantastic insights, reflecting on life and on their pursuit. The top five are "I wish I'd had the courage to live a life true to myself, not the life others expected of me"; "I wish I hadn't worked so hard"; "I wish I'd had the courage to express my feelings"; "I wish I had stayed in touch with my friends"; and "I wish I had let myself be happier."[33,34]

None of these regrets mention money. However, what is also *never* mentioned in these observations about life is that while there's no mention of money, none explicitly say, "I wish I would've made less money," or "I wish money wasn't so important to me." Popular author Daniel Pink's book *The Power of Regret: How Looking Backward Moves Us Forward,* in its 14 chapters and research, doesn't channel direct accounts of money regrets. So, while much cultural emphasis is given to the idea that nobody has money regrets during and at the end of life, we also must emphasize why it doesn't come up.

Most summary conclusions about regret are that admitting and acknowledging regret is an expression of necessary reflection to identify what could have been done better, to grab hold of gratitude, and to help live a fuller life, be more present, and make choices with both the present and future in mind. When folks don't mention money directly, they may emphasize *how* they went about life. It's not that they didn't want the resources, opportunities, or human and financial investments that money provides. It's that they wish they would have gone about it differently.

MASTERING YOUR MONEY MINDSET USING THE ATTITUDE OF GRATITUDE

With an attitude of gratitude through an audited mind, money, and spirit, we can now move forward with solutions. Through the nonclinical approach to blending financial planning decisions with psychological theories and science, financial therapy applies psychology frameworks to the "think," "feel," and "behave" journeys of our emotions and actions around money.

The American Psychological Association conducts an annual study on stressors, and money is a top stressor every year. In the 2023 study, 82% of 18–34-year-olds reported money stress, 77% of 35–44-year-olds reported money stress, and 63% of 45–64-year-olds reported money stress.[35,36] The same study revealed that many people don't want to even talk about money. Making money is *still* a taboo subject among family, friends, and spouses. Communicating about your money can be a positive start and a sustainer of a commitment to well-being and compassion with your finances and life goals. One way to begin communicating about your money is to grab hold of an attitude of gratitude.

The word *gratitude* shows up everywhere, so let's define it. Gratitude is thankfulness and happiness about receiving a gift, whether it be a tangible gift from someone or from happenstance.[37] Through teaching and practice, gratitude can be developed into a sense of personal agency. The virtues of the belief suggest that people have the personal agency to make life better for themselves and persist through adversity and in doing so produce positive outcomes while appreciating pleasant circumstances in the present.

Similarly, faith is a personal topic that everyone holds dear to their heart. Having your own personal relationship with faith is yours, so in this book, when we say *faith*, we mean *faith as you define it*. Faith gives you life every day; you have two feet on the ground, and you are six feet above the ground – or what I like to call two feet on and six feet above. You are given a gift of that day, and appreciating it is a form of gratitude. You have the opportunity to do the best with your given abilities that day. Some days, your best is to get through to the next day. Other days, you are meant to maximize your day to meet your bold aspirations.

It is here where the attitude of gratitude helps your life and money. Research has shown that gratitude helps increase psychological and social well-being.[38]

GRATITUDE IMPROVES EMOTIONAL INTELLIGENCE

1. Increases overall subjective well-being
2. Has positive effects and desirable life outcomes
3. Reduces negative effects and undesirable life outcomes
4. Has positive effects on emotion and mood
5. Lowers stress and anxiety
6. Results in higher levels of empathy and forgiveness
7. Encourages willingness to help others
8. Improves self-esteem

If praying doesn't do it for you, try journaling. Journaling can help you activate gratitude by writing what you're thankful for.[39] In your daily practice, as with any habit, consistency is key. Try expressing your gratitude for 21 days in a row, and then reflect on how your overall well-being has changed from where you started. Your attitude, gratitude, and journaling will lead to discovering your life and money aspirations and identifying the actions you need to take to create the life that you want.

START YOUR SOLUTIONS-BASED STRATEGY

Solutions-focused Behavioral Therapy (SFBT) allows people to be forward thinking, promotes finding solutions for the present, and inspires people with hope and willingness to improve their life design going forward.[40] In most instances, asking the right questions in the right way helps unlock those answers we seek most. Professional practitioners using SFBT suggest that this journey prepares you for the change that you walk yourself into acknowledging and are willing to make. Using explorative questions that focus on asking yourself *instead*, *miracle* and *tomorrow* prompts will reveal your preferred life, both for now and moving forward.

The LMB questions help you find your music notes to bring harmony – a place of mindfulness and readiness of action – by bringing your journey to the present and looking forward to the future with the right balance. You can hear the joyous sound of your clapperboard snapping you into action.

LIFE MONEY BALANCE QUESTIONS

Here's your miracle setup. Imagine having financial security and no negative trade-off between your ideal current and future self. Answer these questions:

1. What "experiences" events would you like to do more frequently?
2. What "well-being services" would you purchase to increase your quality of life?
3. What quality or luxury goods would you like to purchase soon that would contribute to your quality of life?
4. Using the LMB wheel, what value domain resonates with you the most when assigning your present dollars?

What Does Action Have to Do with the Money?

The admitting and acknowledgment stage clears your soul to act. The action stage begins with preparation and a belief that the solutions for your future can be dreamed of and achieved. During this stage, the soul is deep in the process of experiencing forgiveness and giving oneself permission to move forward, to believe in the worthiness of living abundantly and thriving.

One key step at the beginning of the action stage, which we will revisit during the alignment and achievement stages, is identifying those areas that you specifically do not want to do anymore, that are costing you energy and money. Remember your stories and statements? An attainable action step at this point is to pull a 90-day statement and identify the life and money events that no longer align with where you want to go or that no longer fulfill your well-being. The results are the specific areas of "don't wants." Presto! Immediately, you have found money to assign toward desirable LMB domains and facets and in doing so have increased your well-being. You've identified activities and events that don't bring you joy. Readiness and willingness, belief, and self-esteem are all worth money!

Let's say you've identified several patterns of overspending in areas of overindulgence or emotional spending in areas that lack fulfillment. Ask yourself, "Did these events, goods, services, actions, and dollars spent contribute to my overall well-being now or for my future?" "How do they make me feel?" "What do I want currently and in the future now that I've done the work of the first two steps of the honest self-audit?" Those are real questions representing real dollars! That is real well-being! You have now found dollars to invest in your quality of life, in your preferred domains.

This step of efficacy, which is having control of your current and future and how you want to live, is priceless. Now that you have reshaped your perspective of what you can't, shouldn't, or haven't been doing, according to your own terms, you seize more control. You now feel more prepared for those roll-and-adapt events that may come along in life. How good does that feel?

Of course, much must be done between when an airplane leaves the gate and approaches the runway for takeoff. The plane begins motion, backing out from the gate and driving toward the runway. These are small but essential steps of action before taking off at high speeds and flying the friendly skies to your next destination.

KEY TAKEAWAYS

- The life and money action stage requires mindfulness and a solutions focus, helping you move from stagnation to striving.
- Solutions-focused Behavioral Therapy (SFBT) allows people to be forward-thinking, promotes finding solutions for the present,

and inspires people with hope and willingness to improve their life design going forward.

- Identify the life and money events that no longer align with where you want to go or that no longer fulfill your well-being. Find dollars to invest in your quality of life and your preferred domains.
- Use mindfulness and gratitude to bring about, support, and sustain an action mindset and movements.

Journal to Find Your Financial Harmony

Feelings + Finances helps your Finances Flourish. Take time to reflect on the takeaways in this chapter. Enjoy your time and journal only what connects with you most. Any findings during your journaling discovery will help you activate the Five-Point Life Planning Process.

- What life and money themes in this chapter speak specifically to your journey?
- Can you identify opportunities in your feelings and finances to align your life and money aspirations better, giving your money assignments to achieve the life you want?
- Were there any messages in the chapter that helped you:
  - Shake social money stigmas.
  - Release or address money anxiety, judgment, or shame.
  - Move toward better security and understanding of your finances.
  - Find more contentment or fulfillment or want to find some.
  - Discover or improve your relationship with money.
- Scan the Life Money Balance® Wheel, the Six-A-Alignment System™, and the Humanity of Money™. Did content in the chapter help you see yourself in a life stage, season, preference, domain, aspiration, money goal, or mindset?

Journaling Page

_____

_____

_____

_____

_____

_____

_____

_____

_____

_____

_____

_____

_____

_____

_____

_____

CHAPTER FIVE

ALIGNING MONEY WITH VALUES

GOLDEN TIME OF DAY

Aligning your money with your values is the beginning of the fun part of finding your harmony. The *Oprah* show went through a product giveaway phase where, like her famous Oprah's Book Club, if your products received a product endorsement on the Oprah Show, sales went through the roof, and you experienced the "Oprah Effect."[41] The effect turned unknowns into TV personalities and small business owners into millionaires; it produced 59 *USA Today* Top 10 bestsellers with 22 reaching number one on the valued list.[42]

The most fun part of the giveaway shows was when Ms. Winfrey would surprise the audience by asking them to look under their seats for an envelope for the big reveal. She would enthusiastically announce the prize, put two hands in the air like a referee signaling a touchdown, and scream in a high, angelic tenor, "Ahhhhhhhh!" It was a fun "Ahh!" moment. The first three A's in the Six-A Financial Harmony System are an awakening "Ahh!" moment. For the system, it looks like AAA moments with short "A" sounds: admit, acknowledge, act. If you've made it this far, you know the feeling is glorious; you get to begin the next step of the Six-A Financial Harmony System, aligning your life with your money to create the life you envision.

THE SCIENCE OF SELF

Exploring alignment is finding your unique identity. Although not the driver of discovering your values, a "fun fact" is that almost everyone enjoys talking about themselves. Communication, like emotion, is a pillar of human connection and central to social connection. Reports find that 60% of conversations are filled with self-talk, moving to 80% when communicating through social media platforms.[43] Science and studies support a commonsense revelation about self-talk: talking about yourself feels good.

Harvard University researchers at their neuroscience lab used magnetic resonance imaging to examine the self-talk effect.[43] When the researchers asked two groups questions about their opinions and their personality traits, the group that answered the questions about themselves had higher neural activation than the group that answered in relation to others. Another revelation is that the areas of the brain stimulated were the prefrontal cortex, nucleus accumbens, and the ventral tegmental areas – the former responsible for self-thought and the latter two activating the mesolimbic dopamine system.

The dopamine system is the reward system that activates pleasure and motivation states, with links to stimuli such as sex, comfort food, and cocaine. So, after someone finishes talking about themself, you can ask them, "Was it good for you?" Jokes aside, when someone asks you about you, there's reason for joy!

ALIGNING THE PERSON WITH PROSPERITY IN YOUR FINANCIAL PLAN

The *process* of planning your finances has set aside space for life and money alignment and discovering what you value most. The first two of the seven steps of the financial planning process as defined by the CFP Board are first, understanding the client's personal and financial circumstances, and second, identifying and selecting goals.[44] In this second step, subjective qualitative and objective quantitative information is gathered. It's key to note the undertones of the "big words." Qualitative information is quality-of-life data; quantitative is the information you can quantify or count. The count data at the macro level are, but not limited to, your savings, investments, income, revenue, equity, benefits, estate, retirement savings rates, assets, liabilities, and net worth. The first two steps are where dollars and senses begin to intersect across the life stage to represent the whole self.

The quality-of-life data includes your values, attitudes, perceptions, and goals. It extends further to money psychology areas, including your experiences, culture, beliefs, and emotions across life and your relationships with money. When you hear about how to manage your finances, independently or with a professional, the transformative system and financial journey is a wholeness equation to prosperity.

FIVE-POINT LIFE PLANNING PROCESS

Person + Preferences + Purpose + Points + Plan = Prosperity

The LMB philosophy of *letting your life lead your money where your life and money work concurrently to achieve your life design* translates to finding your harmony, interweaving all relevant elements of your finances to your life. Here, you can begin to align your life and money value systems; it will forge the value you place in the process and the outcomes it will produce.

UNDERSTANDING THE MONEY'S SIGNIFICANT ROLE IN YOUR JOURNEY

The essential part of the Humanity of Money is the everyday interconnectedness of money in the emotions and events across your life stages. The conversation and exploration of the role money plays in our internal life can be tough and, *externally*, can spur social shame. Gather trusted financial education about money and align your unique value system with your money to develop your *internal* relationship with money. Because money touches *every* part of our existence, we must acknowledge its vital role and impact.

Stigmas to money may contribute to how we handle our finances and earn and align money with our journey. You may have heard that "your net worth is not your self-worth," "the love of money is the root of all evil," "money can't buy happiness," "experiences are more valuable than things," "live within your means," "it's not all about the money," "life is more than money," or "wants vs. needs."

Significant studies on unconscious money beliefs that we learn through direct or indirect experiences with money during childhood, or social influences that develop our beliefs and behaviors that contribute to self-destructive or counterproductive life and money outcomes, are called money scripts.[45] The Money Scripts Inventory (MSI) is a well-meaning and respected assessment developed by scholarly researchers that places due importance on the need to investigate limiting beliefs that could hinder your life and money progress. The MSI identifies areas where conversations, additional objective information, and insight encourage self-inspired adjustments for healing that can influence better outcomes.

The four money script domains are Money Status, Money Vigilance, Money Avoidance, and Money Worship. Folks may have traits in all four scripts, yet one script may dominate. Learned beliefs from environments beyond one's control are one thing; societal influences stemming from interpretations carried as social norms are another and may disrupt a healthy relationship with money and potentially shame an otherwise uniquely logical life and money alignment.

Both may hinder life and money alignment and be barriers to aspirational progress. However, the influence of society and social norms is where information, educators, academics, and professionals can do better to help assist your alignment with money. These can support your journey instead of adding strain and shame as you strive for empowered understanding so you can flourish.

WANTS ARE NEEDS, TOO! STATUS IS A WANT

Consider the struggle inherent in the conflicting dynamics of *status*. There is social capital in status. In Maslow's Hierarchy of Needs[46,47,48], people are motivated to reach their highest level of self-actualization through their life's lens, represented by a triangle. The bottom two foundations of the triangle are physiological "needs," and the stack on top are psychological "wants." The want levels are love and belonging, esteem, and self-actualization. While Maslow's triangle may not be strictly ordinal from bottom to top, the journey navigating the triangle is interconnected to what people need and want for their life, how they want, and what they value most.

The esteem section contains respect, self-esteem, recognition, strength, and freedom. Most experts and many people misinterpret that life's journey is *holistic*—Integrated Life Stage Well-Being, the formal name LMB— it's not needs *or* wants; it's needs *and* wants. You see, wants are needs, too! They are an interdependent system toward realizing your whole self.

You may often hear the phrase that your "net worth is not your self-worth." Folks who rate money status highly in their money scripts equate the two. If you wake up every day and your *only* measuring stick for your self-worth is money, yes, that maladaptive behavior rather than a purposeful life will contribute to self-destructive behaviors such as overspending or impulse spending, wreaking havoc on a financial plan and your well-being.

However, investing in status as a *wholeness* domain is about belonging and connecting with your networks—positive ingredients for prospering. While some people spend to "keep up with the Joneses" or suffer from the need to impress others for self-fulfillment, the counter side is that folks are investing in their overall esteem. Two esteem and status sayings come to mind. One is Deion Sanders's famous line, "If you look good, you feel good. If you feel good, you play good. If you play good, they pay good," which is a combination of preference and esteem of the self, *not* an outward need to impress. The other is mine: while your "self-worth is *not* your net worth, your self-worth *helps make* your net worth."

Esteem and status interplay. Those with higher self-esteem have higher net worth.[49,50] Your social circle and network matter, which is good economically and emotionally, making status an investment in your holistic self. Nobel Prize Winner in Economics Gary Becker suggests in his Social

Interaction Theory that people's social environment increases their ability to produce output and thus income to maximize their well-being.[51]

Your status domain can be a wealth, well-being, social, and overall advancement asset. However, social stigma has warped the interpretation of status attainment as a character defect. However, keeping your network is not your self-worth crutch if you don't determinately worship it. Adhering to biased thinking can deter folks from the purposeful pursuit of money to advance their human condition, contributing to a shortcoming of life and money aspirations. Ironically, not recognizing what status means in the healthy hierarchy of self creates an opportunity to erroneously plug into the prevalent "humble money" social capital by acting as if "status is bad" *solely* to avoid appearing like a maladjusted human being.

WEALTH AND WELL-BEING ARE DIFFERENT

Wealth and well-being are different, but they are dancing partners to the same song. In the 2023 Modern Wealth Study by Charles Schwab,[52] folks were asked which statements best describe wealth and how to think of wealth as a monetary or nonmonetary description. Most chose a non-monetary statement leaning toward well-being. An example would be "having a fulfilling life" compared to "not having to stress over money," or "enjoying experiences." In another section, the same folks were asked what net worth an American would need to feel wealthy – about $2.2 million.[52]

When asked about this, people did not lump wealth and well-being together, but the respondents knew how much money, or wealth, it would take to fund their secure well-being confidently. One is an amount of money; the other is a state of being. Wealth is having an abundance of money or a plentiful amount of something. The two definitions of the term *wealth* are easy to conflate because, by definition, you can have a wealth of knowledge, time, and so on.

However, even by the second definition, the investment, building, and distribution of wealth require vast amounts of time, depth of experience, and generosity. Not separating wealth and well-being discounts the importance of money's role in our lives: wealth funds your preferred well-being state. In short, wealth buys well-being. Said more recognizably, *money buys happiness.* Shocking, I know! We will talk more about this in Chapter 6.

Accumulating wealth, still one of the highest social stigmas because of its illogical alignment to belief systems, is essential to achieving the life you want. If wealth is stigmatized, wealth and well-being become blended to soften the stigma. Some folks might not intentionally seek to build the assets necessary for well-being. Forming a blended view of well-being to be better viewed, internally or externally, as one who understands the "true meaning of money" could shortchange your wealth *and* well-being prospects.

Grab hold of your well-being dreams! Along with aligning your money beliefs, you must align your aspirations to your money; this is the connective glue to your entire financial plan.

What Does Aligning Finances with What You Value Most Have to Do with Money?

Shaking off the shackles of money shame is essential to developing toward your money values. Everyone only has 12 notes to build their song; why cut your note sheet in half with shame? Use all of your notes!

Money provides for a prosperous life, but money has a priority in life, and this is where the confusion comes from. When money becomes the center of a person and is worshiped before everything else, that's when money becomes destructive to a person across all human domains socially, psychologically, spiritually, and financially. However, building wealth with people's purpose, process, and plan in mind is a healthy value system that can fund human flourishing.

It's imperative that you establish value systems that are unique to your personal journey and use trusted information grounded by evidence or sound philosophical theory, independent of noise and misinterpretations. Shaky information and foundations make an already uncertain life and money journey more anxiety ridden. I call that anxiety stacking.

There is no shortage of studies saying people have anxiety about their finances coupled with mistrust about the information available about our finances, bringing us doubt about whether we are doing things correctly on top of our internal self-doubt. Finances are a struggle, so finding *Wealth in the Key of Life* is transformational and freeing.

STEERING YOUR LIFE MONEY BALANCE WHEEL

When it comes to values, let's look at the three dimensions of the LMB Integrated Life Stages to Well-Being – LSU, LCU, and MSU – where you can turn social norms from shaming to shine.

LIFE-CENTERED UTILITY + LIFESTYLE UTILITY

In the area of LCU, experiences and time get a lot of attention. Media and experts say these areas are more important than accumulating things, sometimes serving as sage wisdom. However, this notion is sometimes used as a lecture.

It's as though the people who value more experiences and time are more enlightened and automatically have a higher level of self-actualization and a better understanding of financial literacy and well-being, which may not always be true. Life and money are personal; there's a difference between *Instagram reel* life and *real* life.

Experiences and time cost money, as does lifestyle utility. Everything inside and across all the well-being domains is a preference and requires investment; the domains are personal to the individual – at that point in time and in that person's life.

Take a camping trip. Yes, you can go camping at a low cost. You can take your own vehicle to your local park with a cheap tent and food from your home, take your family out, and have a memorable time. You may say that your family will remember that for the rest of their lives – and that very well may be true.

There are also camping trips at regional, state, or national parks that require big trucks, expensive tents, clothing, propane, fishing boats, rides, coolers, sleeping bags, maybe camper's payments to enter parks, and the vacation time off from businesses and jobs to enjoy the trip. These experiences cost money. It's ridiculous when people say that experiences are more important than things, as though experiences don't cost money and they don't have money life values. Money is more than *just* a tool. Money is a *partner* because a partner has a *soul*. A partner is essential and is part of life's existence. Recall from our introduction in the "Music of Your Money" section.

WEALTH IN THE KEY OF LIFE

Your "Key of Life" is a system of integrated sounds that plays to the soul of your life and finances. Your soul is your total self, representing your unique essence, principles, and spirit. Finding harmony, keys, and melodies is essential to shaping your life's design and finances.

LIFE-CENTERED UTILITY

Time has a cost as well. I love a good old-fashioned time value of money (TVM) calculator, whether it be a Hewlett-Packard (HPII+) or a Texas Instruments (BAII+) calculator. There are diehard calculator-type enthusiasts. You can use TVM for online calculators or plain Excel software. Whatever your tool of choice, you'll find the measurement for a popular yet unpopular phrase: *time is money*. You can't buy more lifetime, but you can buy more quality time. In other words, time affluence. There's an associated cost when you buy, waste, or spend time. Remember, wealth funds well-being, and both require time, the former to build and the latter to enjoy.

NBA basketball star Rasheed Wallace was at the free throw line in a basketball game, famously arguing a bad foul call with a referee. An opposing basketball player was shooting a free throw and missed the shot. Rasheed yelled out, "Ball don't lie!" Well, the time value of money calculators and math don't lie. As young people say nowadays, "That math ain't mathing!"

Time has a cost in the form of future or present value across time. Folks have time preferences through time discounting, where individuals can value the future or the present more. This means they can choose to discount the value of the future by living more now or choose to live more in the future, producing a trade-off cost.

Time also has risk costs that we can measure through interest rates, whether in bonds, mortgages, or CD rates. The longer the time horizon, the higher the interest rate. Again, time has its cost. Nobel Prize–winning economic theorist Gary Becker used Household Economics Theory to demonstrate the cost of time.[51] In a coupled household in which two people's talents are measured in the market, if the household chooses to use both talents to produce financial incomes and buy goods and services (such as groceries or cleaning), great. However, the household could also choose to select one spouse's higher financial income and instead use the time of the other spouse for goods and services because that pairing delivers the highest output and well-being for that household.

When people say that they value time with their family over things, it is not something they should be saying out of bravado or as though they are expressing better values or financial literacy practices over others. This book practices not having directive shaming *shoulds*. Having financial access to purchase time should be an expression of gratitude. That's why money is not just a tool; it's a partner with a soul and is an essential part of our existence.

In the example given, either two people are using their finances to purchase goods and services for more time, or one person has their finances, and the other is utilizing their talents to provide the time to transfer as a gift and thus an expression of gratitude.

LIFE-STYLE UTILITY

Let's discuss LSU, specifically tangible goods. LSU is a domain that's experienced differently across life stages. For example, in your early or mid-stages of life, social circles, status, and networks may carry strong importance for you. During these stages, a first-time experience or certain material items have more meaning and carry more weight than during other life stages. It doesn't make you wrong or shallow. It just means that you may not have had access to them before, but now that you have the means, you are expressing your preferences that you may not have had the capability to express before.

When you hear someone say that a material item doesn't mean that much to them anymore, have they already had the experience with it? Or don't they already have it? Would they give the comfort of the goods and services back? What is *really* being said when material items are "not as important as experiences and people?" What is the priority and purpose behind those purchases? What were they for? Why were they purchased? Who were they trying to impress?

Quality and even luxury goods and services that support your well-being and quality of life are perfectly okay! These purchases fit the LMB Integrated Life Stage Well-Being continuum and the Five-Point Life Planning Process. You can live in the prosperity you deserve, within your plan and preferences!

BE YOU WITHOUT EXPLANATION WHILE WORKING YOUR PLAN

A study by researchers at the University of Colorado suggests there's a stigma attached to those who purchase material items even when those material items are purchased for intrinsic value.[53] In other words, items purchased for intrinsic value are purchased to support quality of life and happiness, not for external motivations. Moreover, there is a stigma against material purchasers compared to experiential purchasers, as though materialistic purchasers possess unfavorable value systems or, in the study's words, "unfavorable impressions."

When you are in the airport, you always hear the announcement to "keep your eye on your own luggage!" It's the same when you are aligning your life and money values to give your money assignments. Your life and money are yours and yours only. Within the context of the prosperity formula, you are responsible for your bags! Tell everyone else to watch their own luggage.

KEY TAKEAWAYS

- Wealth and well-being are different, but they are dancing partners to the same song.
- Accumulating wealth, still one of the highest social stigmas because of its illogical alignment to belief systems, is essential to achieving the life you want.
- Time is money. You can't buy more lifetime, but you can buy more quality time.
- Money provides for a prosperous life, but money has a priority in life, which is where the confusion comes from.
- You must establish value systems that are unique to your personal journey.

Journal to Find Your Financial Harmony

Feelings + Finances helps your Finances Flourish. Take time to reflect on the takeaways in this chapter. Enjoy your time and journal only what connects with you most. Any findings during your journaling discovery will help you activate the Five-Point Life Planning Process.

- What life and money themes in this chapter speak specifically to your journey?
- Can you identify opportunities in your feelings and finances to align your life and money aspirations better, giving your money assignments to achieve the life you want?
- Were there any messages in the chapter that helped you:
  - Shake social money stigmas.
  - Release or address money anxiety, judgment, or shame.
  - Move toward better security and understanding of your finances.
  - Find more contentment or fulfillment or want to find some.
  - Discover or improve your relationship with money.
- Scan the Life Money Balance® Wheel, the Six-A-Alignment System™, and the Humanity of Money™. Did content in the chapter help you see yourself in a life stage, season, preference, domain, aspiration, money goal, or mindset?

Journaling Page

CHAPTER SIX

ASPIRING FOR FINANCIAL FREEDOM

The only goal I've ever heard delivered with the soul of life is when the world-renowned sports anchor and television personality Andres Cantor belts out "Goooooooooooal!" when a goal is scored in soccer matches. Being goals oriented helps build a system of measurable and meaningful action, accountability, and definable achievements. The songbook of aspiration is written when you arrange your notes and keys, creating your life album of songs. Aspirations and goals are different, but they partner to get you where you want to go.

Your unique life aspirations are like a timeless, no-skip record that you want to keep playing across your life's course because it touches you deeply. There are endless lists of the top records of all time; these are classics. A few come to mind:

Thriller (Micheal Jackson, 1982)

The Dark Side of the Moon (Pink Floyd, 1973)

Songs in the Key of Life (Stevie Wonder, 1976),

What's Going On (Marvin Gaye, 1971),

Back to Black (Amy Winehouse, 2006)

Jagged Little Pill (Alanis Morissette, 1995)

Illmatic (Nas, 1994)

Nevermind (Nirvana, 1991)

Come On Over (Shania Twain, 1997)

Kind of Blue (Miles Davis, 1959)

Like many best-of-all-time records lists, yours will be subjective and unique to the way art affects your soul. But one common aspect that will be the same across these albums will be quality. What aspect of life and money is timeless, unique to you, and yet similar across humanity in its effect on advancing your condition? Aspiration.

LIVE YOUR ASPIRATIONAL LIFE

All financial plans are life plans. *Creating* the life you want is the most pivotal part of the LMB® journey. Starting and understanding any journey, especially your financial plan, helps discover your "why." To live ASPRTNLY is *living* the life you want the most, which brings you fulfillment!

QUESTIONS TO LIVE ASPRTNLY™

You gain clarity and confidence and determine with certainty what you do and don't want to do. Making a change, committing to the process, and living the life you want must come from a strong eagerness for change, where you feel there's no other alternative to how you want to live!

HERE ARE QUESTIONS TO ASK YOURSELF:

1. What do you aspire to do?
2. What is the meaning and purpose of what you want to do?
3. Why is your *why* central to your existence?
4. How is your *why* intimately linked to your unique identity, values, experiences, and culture?
5. What are you willing to do to achieve them?

Aspirations are different from goals. Aspirations are bold and courageous desires that reflect how you want to live your life now and in the future.[54] Think of aspirations as your hope and realistic dreams and goals as your actions to attain and sustain your ideal life. Do not let the parameters of realism become a limiting belief or result in an aspiration not being pursued.

FINDING YOUR WHOLE IDEAL SELF

Ask yourself, "Why am I not living my ideal life" or "Why am I not being my ideal self?" Your aspirations should be so strong that you feel motivated to live the life you want fully. There are two types of aspirations: intrinsic and extrinsic.[54] Intrinsic aspirations help satisfy psychological desires to pursue your best version of self, life, and well-being. Extrinsic aspirations focus on achieving a grand desired outcome. These are the top three sections of Maslow's Triangle of Human Motivation to achieve your best self and possess the personal motivation to align with your current self – your ideal life. The world continuously rotates on its axis, creating the energy of life. Your LMB® Wheel rotates across life's course to generate the continuum of energy integrating your preference-driven well-being domains and finances and producing the wealth-secured life you want – your aspirational life.

You need both intrinsic and extrinsic aspirations. Intrinsic aspirations focus on meaning and purpose, such as engaging in family and friend relationships and having good physical and mental health. Intrinsic aspiration can be connection based, such as getting married and having children, or can reflect personal growth aspirations, such as career, business, or educational pursuits.

Extrinsic examples are goals like financial freedom or wealth goals centering on certain amounts or social status. Some studies suggest that people who are more *intrinsically* inclined have healthier and more self-aware pursuits, while *financially aspirational* folks may have higher amounts of stress and anxiety.

Here again, social constructs with the support of misinterpreted or misapplied science or study may lead folks away from financial or wealth aspirations when hearing "life is more than money" or "it's not all about the money." Because of repeated suggestions by society, professionals, and "gurus," people may discount money's significant role in funding our life aspirations and well-being.

What studies demonstrate, but don't emphasize, is that if people have money and wealth aspirations that are *purely* motivated by connecting their self-worth to net worth or other subjective financial success, then *that* behavior is mostly self-destructive and self-defeating. However, having an *aspiration* to attain a certain amount of money to achieve *financial freedom, independent* of the pursuit of self-worth, is *not* unhealthy.

MONEY BUYS HAPPINESS

Here's the "wealth funds well-being" discussion. There are popular and oft empirically researched or poll-studied questions on the minds of many. *Does money buy happiness?* Your well-being is highly important to your journey's quality, meaning, fulfillment, and contentment and is central to this book. Your overall well-being is essentially your happiness. You can identify and invest in your happiness. Yes, *money buys happiness!*

Let's unpack *happiness* and *well-being*, terms used interchangeably throughout this book. You must understand how to align your life and money and assign your dollars to the life you want without shame, guilt, regret, or explanation.

From the dictionary and economic definitions, you'll find a connection to how you identify what will increase your well-being or happiness through feelings of satisfaction, contentment, and joy. In economics, these feelings of happiness are the utility you receive from goods and services. If you think of happiness as the unit you can purchase by using your dollars to purchase the goods and services necessary to produce your preferred happiness or well-being state, then your money can buy happiness!

With proper context, *happiness* and *well-being* can be used interchangeably. When people hear that money buys happiness, folks immediately jump to feelings of euphoria or pleasant smiles, love, and laughter. That may only sometimes be the case. Units of happiness – well-being – increase your broader quality of life in the domain area you value most or need the most at the life stage.

For example, say you have persistent back pain requiring back surgery and your pain level is 10. The back surgery brings your back pain to 4, where zero is having no back pain. Having zero back pain would probably bring you that dream sequence feeling of happiness everyone defaults to. Although level 4 back pain is still pain, your well-being or happiness level

HAPPINESS

The *feeling* of being *happy*;

WELL-BEING

The state of *feeling healthy* and happy

SATISFACTION

A pleasant *feeling* that you get when you receive something you wanted or when you have done something you wanted to do

OTHER SYNONYMS OF HAPPINESS

Contentment, joy

UTILITY

Economics refers to the usefulness, satisfaction, or enjoyment a consumer can get from a service or good.

is increased, and you allocate your *available* dollars to purchase units of happiness. Without money for insurance or out-of-pocket expenses, there's no surgery, and your happiness level is stuck at back pain 10 – *wealth funds well-being.*

In 2010, a study by Nobel Peace Prize–winning economist from Princeton, Daniel Kahneman, suggested that happiness rose as income increased to $75,000, then after $75,000, happiness began to level off and increase less with each additional dollar.[55] I don't know about you, but through personal experience and experiences with clients I've served, I see much that folks value in their LMB Wheel that can be purchased with dollars above this amount. A different Ivy League study thought so, too! In 2021, the University of Pennsylvania's Matthew Killingsworth published research suggesting that happiness increased handily with incomes well beyond $ 75,000 with no plateau in sight.[55] Who's right?

Both researchers came together to investigate the matter and publish a joint study, and here's what they found. They were both *right* – this time with added context and broader interpretation. Here's an example of why there's an enormous responsibility to conduct and contribute evidence-based literature with thoughtful interpretation that will impact social norms. Their findings? In general, *there is ever-increasing happiness for people with higher incomes beyond $100,000* — one catch: happiness peaks for a group of "miserable" folks around $100,000. People at or above this amount are considered "well-off," but if you are already unhappy, money won't help.

The outcome of the "adversarial collaboration" work reveals a critical element to happiness. It would be best to discover what you value most – what brings you *happiness* (fulfillment, well-being, joy, contentment, satisfaction) – first and along the way so you can use your dollars to purchase more units of happiness. *Yes, money can buy happiness!* – IF you courageously and boldly do the work to discover what your units of happiness are. Without doing the work in the Six-A Financial Harmony System, you are miserable, and no amount of money will bring you happiness.

Clearly identifying and better understanding your intrinsic aspirations for meaning, fulfillment, and purpose – your *why* – and partnering your intrinsic aspiration with your external aspiration, specifically financial, can produce healthy outcomes. When the LMB® philosophy tells you to let your life lead your money, having a sound understanding of your aspirations will give you purpose, meaning, fulfillment, and well-being. Concurrently, you aspire to engage in attitudes, behavior, and actions to pursue and generate the financial wealth you need to fund what matters most to you.

It's perfectly okay to have intrinsic and extrinsic aspirations; perhaps there is no need to distinguish them when healthily aligned. They are unified aspirations that require goals-based frameworks to achieve them.

THE LMB® WHEEL AND THE 8 DIMENSIONS OF WELLNESS

Life and financial aspirations exist in the same circle system of needs. Dr. Margaret (Peggy) Swarbrick developed the 8 Dimensions of Wellness to help people recover from mental health and substance abuse trauma.[56] The Dimensions are now used broadly as a framework supporting the pursuit of thriving in human wholeness.

The premise is that the emotional, spiritual, intellectual, environmental, physical, social, vocational, and financial dimensions are connected and that while each dimension doesn't have to be equal, there must be harmony among them to find your version of contentment.[57,58] Whether you have a negative fundamental belief toward money, you use your financial dimension to fund your other dimensions, and the financial dimension is no less important than others. You have your own permission to pursue your aspirations, including those in your money dimension, without shame, judgment, or doubt that you are doing the "right thing" for your well-being as you define it.

Remember that wants are needs, too! Wants are aspirational domains toward your fullest life and are required to achieve your whole self. That's why the "want" domains often feel like must-dos instead of wants, making them needs. The aspiration to be your whole self is the essence and existence of life, of your soul, making your finances the humanity of money. Your motivation to achieve your full self, including your finances, is within you. Your humanity of money requires an investment, and is why the management and the attainment of "more" until you reach "more than enough" is essential.

THE ENOUGH PARADOX

"The Enough Paradox" puzzles many people, including professional financial advisors, wellness professionals, and gurus. Understanding your "enough" directly impacts your aspirational journey, and getting good with your enough helps shape your aspirations. There are two parts of the enough paradox folks tend to struggle with most. One is the audacity to hold their thoughts of enough without apology, and the other is the fear of misunderstanding enough. It's okay. Your measure of enough is yours.

I probably just confused the living daylights out of you. Let's make it plain because your enough questions are valid.

COMMON "ENOUGH" QUESTIONS

- "Do I have enough?"
- "Will I have enough?"
- "Have I had enough?"

YOUR "ENOUGH" WHILE SAVING FOR RETIREMENT OR INVESTING IN YOUR CURRENT SELF

- "Will I (we) have enough money to fund my (our) aspirational life?"

YOUR "ENOUGH" QUESTION DURING RETIREMENT

- "Do I (we) have enough money to fund my (our) aspirational life?"

It's okay to put "money" at the end of those first three questions. The word *money* evokes emotional reactions when spoken aloud. It may raise those inner-self questions or conditional labels, "Am I thinking just about money?" "Am I making money part of my self-worth?" "Am I bad for thinking about money?" No, you are not. It's okay to want more money until you have "more than enough."

If your aspiration is "I want to achieve financial freedom," and the motivation is supported by your *whys* – "so that I can travel, consult part-time in a globally neutral location, have another child, level up our lifestyle utility, hike in the mountains, spend more time with family, maintain our lifestyle comfort, live in a traveling RV for a couple of years, start a band, become an author, confidently retire" – you are doing two things with this approach.

Firstly, you can assign a dollar amount to your aspirations, and secondly, you have aligned your money with internal aspirations and not your self-worth or external validation. Evidence shows that purpose in life contributes to higher levels of income and net worth.[59] Your "more money" matters when it is tied to what matters more – to you.

Technically, there will never be enough money. You don't know when you are going to die. Longevity risk is the risk of outliving your money. Uncertainty is certain, so you don't know the magnitude of unexpected events, and you will always wonder if you are managing your money and lifestyle to fund your lifestyle and retirement. With a better understanding of your aspirations and the goals that align with attainment, you will gain more clarity and confidence in your enough. You will make statements like "I've had enough of this sh*t," "Enough is enough," and "I have enough" – declarative because you've painted your picture and you know your canvas space is filled.

BELIEVE ABUNDANCE IS FOR YOU: FLOURISH WITH YOUR FINANCES

Another key element to living your fullest life is believing you can design and live your preferred life, and believing you are worthy of living abundantly, flourishing both with your finances and your soul. How you investigate and determine your self-worth and value impacts your beliefs about money attainment and abundance and affects how you use your money to fund your aspirational life. Some studies show that people don't relate to wealth because they don't feel wealthy, the concept of wealth is not for them, or wealth doesn't pertain to their amount of money.[60] Believing your worthiness to having wealth and abundance is different from tying your self-worth to your net worth.

Identifying and imagining your bold aspirations takes courage and conviction; your aspirations require substantial investment and the building of that investment. As a precursor for the audacity to dream big, you must first feel worthy to live abundantly, be prosperous, and live the life you envision.

When you identify your aspirations, they are not just for the distant future. Your aspirations include your current self. Your current self may not be your ideal self, but once identified, you can begin making changes that align both selves. Aspire for your life now and for your life later.

LIVE FULLY NOW AND RETIRE CONFIDENTLY: IT'S *AND*, NOT *OR!*

LSV will contribute to your aspirations and help you weigh tradeoffs. One notion is certain: while delayed gratification has its benefits and helps prevent overspending, impulse spending, and directionless spending, all of which significantly damage your wealth-building journey, you don't have to suffer from deprivation. You don't have to starve your *now* to feed your *later*.

Vitality refers to physical and psychological "aliveness" with physical realms, including capability, health, energy, and psychological realms, including meaning and purpose.[61] Different life stages may contain different preferences, meaning some things may matter more or less than others in different life stages. While still having integrated LMB® well-being dimensions, some domains or facets of those domains may weigh differently in value or purpose to you. Some factors could be bound to a particular life stage, contributing to severe discounting of your time now for future promises and leading to regret.

The terms FOMO (fear of missing out) and YOLO (you only live once) are popular, but what about YODO (you only die once)? Fear of missing out causes you to suffer from the herd mentality, where you blindly follow investment trends and make emotion-driven decisions that may not fit your personal investment policy, risk tolerance, or needs. This makes your finances suboptimal or causes you to suffer from comparing your stuff or journey to others, draining finances and well-being and making you more prone to keeping up with the Joneses or to having self-worth as your net-worth mentality.

YOLO is a severe discounting of your future self, overinvesting in the now due to a belief that the only opportunity you will ever have is now. Since you are not guaranteed the future, why not? Both FOMO and YOLO belief systems promote unhealthy finances and well-being. Your aspirations fit better with YODO. If I possess these vital abilities, I want to fully experience my wishes, dreams, and aspirations because I would feel certain about it if I hadn't been in the life stage where it mattered most. You die once; your aspirational life has a wave of multiple opportunities, and passing on your fair share can lead to unfulfillment.

When you investigate and find inspiration for your aspirations for the life you want now and in the future, you can be free of the burdens of limiting beliefs of self or of social conditioning. Be bold and claim the identity of your best life, independent of external influence.

What Does Financial Freedom Have to Do with Money?

Aspiration is the epitome of why the separation of wealth and well-being is essential. You can have well-being without wealth, which is a preference, but aspirational well-being requires investment, which is also a preference. Two people help clearly explain this state of aspirational being.

FREEDOM IS IN THE EYE OF THE BEHOLDER

We called my mother's mother Grandma (rest her soul). She was one of the freest people I've ever met. She didn't have much money, though she did experience an abundance of money once in her life. Toward the end of her life, she didn't have a wealth of dollars. However, she had one of the highest states of well-being regarding her sense of self. This was by choice; it was a preference, though there were the happenstances of life that affected outcomes along the way.

I can't stress this enough: choices, willpower, positive thinking, hard work, or work ethic alone don't promise positive life and wealth outcomes. There are so many other factors. That said, engaging in many of these things increases your chances of achieving your preferred outcomes. Living with grace and gratitude will magnify these action factors.

Aspiration is to seek something ambitiously, perhaps something of high value. The measurements or interpretations of ambition's great value are particular to the person. From what I can discern from my grandma, one aspiration she had and did well was to be a truth teller, be free from all consequences, and be her own unique person. She did that well, requiring low investment. She also told a hell of a story.

DEFINE WHAT FREEDOM MEANS TO YOU

My father is another person who embodies a combination of wealth and well-being as he defines it. I've repeatedly asked my dad what his greatest aspiration has been. Pops is a BBQ enthusiast. He uses a large custom smoker grill made up of pipe steel that was used to transport oil on the ground – he's that serious. I always thought that his aspiration would be to become wealthy in dollars and be a successful barbecue restaurateur. He shared with me on many occasions and on the LMB® podcast that he's had one aspiration that predated him being a good husband and family man. He said that on the first day he started working, he realized he did not want to work anymore! I laughed the first time I heard this, and I still find it funny.

He aspired to utilize the talent of his dedication and work ethic he learned from his father, and loyalty to his family, and devotion to his wife, alongside the teamwork from my mother to attain their version of "more than enough," to retire. From their "must do to retire" to "what they want to do" – that's what his aspiration was. That is his aspirational well-being, and he knew how much wealth dollars it took to fund that lifestyle.

He and my mother decided they wanted a comfortable, paid-off lifestyle that allowed them to travel just a little bit. Not that they need or want any explanation of themselves, but my parents are not cheap. They have a little bit of style. My Pops has a few custom lizard boots in his closet that he wears when the time calls for them, and both of my parents like quality goods and services, as well as experiences to maximize their quality of life across the domains of the life money balance wheel. They do not deprive themselves of well-being in any of the domains whether it be LSU, MPU, or LCU.

They are very comfortable with who they are and are living with peace of mind. They don't feel they are missing out and don't feel the need to explain how they go about their life to anyone. Anybody who has ever met my father will tell you he is a free person, that he says what he thinks, what he means, and what he feels pretty much at any time, though not to offend anyone. He is financially and aspirationally free, the way he defines it.

ABUNDANT WEALTH AND WELL-BEING ARE FOR YOU!

What does all this have to do with your aspirations? Sure, you can have well-being without wealth. Sure, you can aspire to wealth and well-being that don't seem grand to others but are grand to you; they don't need to be explained to others and they are indeed an abundant life.

However, if it is your preference, you also have the freedom to think boldly about your wealth and well-being aspirations and how you want to create your life design. The life you want can be big and abundant in the literal sense, taking any shape or form you would like, and that, too, is not shameful. You are worthy of abundance, and that, too, requires no explanation.

Everybody likes to dream; aspiration is fun. Dreaming is one of those common traits of humanity, like love, loss, sadness, joy, belonging, and community. Aspiration stokes the fire, and you can put a log on it daily. Direct your dollars in ways that will align and elevate your ideal current self with your future self to create and sustain your best self.

KEY TAKEAWAYS

- Aspirations are bold and courageous desires that reflect how you want to live your life now and in the future.
- Does money buy happiness? Your well-being is highly important to your journey's quality, meaning, fulfillment, and contentment. Yes, *money buys happiness*!
- LSV will contribute to your aspirations and help you weigh trade-offs. One notion is certain: while delayed gratification has benefits, you don't have to starve your *now* to feed your *later*.
- It is okay to want more money until you have "more than enough." But there will never be enough money.
- Believing your worthiness to having wealth and abundance is different from tying your self-worth to your net worth.

Journal to Find Your Financial Harmony

Feelings + Finances helps your Finances Flourish. Take time to reflect on the takeaways in this chapter. Enjoy your time and journal only what connects with you most. Any findings during your journaling discovery will help you activate the Five-Point Life Planning Process.

- What life and money themes in this chapter speak specifically to your journey?
- Can you identify opportunities in your feelings and finances to align your life and money aspirations better, giving your money assignments to achieve the life you want?
- Were there any messages in the chapter that helped you:
  - Shake social money stigmas.
  - Release or address money anxiety, judgment, or shame.
  - Move toward better security and understanding of your finances.
  - Find more contentment or fulfillment or want to find some.
  - Discover or improve your relationship with money.
- Scan the Life Money Balance® Wheel, the Six-A-Alignment System™, and the Humanity of Money™. Did content in the chapter help you see yourself in a life stage, season, preference, domain, aspiration, money goal, or mindset?

Journaling Page

CHAPTER SEVEN

MASTERING FINANCIAL TRIUMPH

S uccess in life and money doesn't always mean transforming trial and trauma into triumph. Realistically, across life's course, you will experience a continuum of the Teas of Life. You can grab hold of achievement by compounding on the motivation energy from your triumphant milestone events. When you are living the life you want, outside of life events you can't control, you have a greater chance to sustain the choices, decisions, and habits that produce triumphant times.

To be triumphant is to be successful or achieve victory, or in the noun sense (triumph), an event, achievement, or victory. The act or achievement of triumph is not produced by a singular element. Reaching the life you want requires an integrated system of events, support, resources, grit, preferences, choices, and hard work. The integrated system I just mentioned sounds a lot like the components of the LMB Integrated Life Stage Well-Being Wheel and supporting theories (see the Introduction).

One key part of achieving your version of life and money success and staying that way is humility, which is to understand the full picture of how you arrive, survive, and thrive in your triumph. There's a lot of talk about "self-made millionaires" from talking heads and popular books. The premise is that being self-made means that these millionaires did not receive a financial inheritance to attain their net worth. Some pundits will say, "Studies show," "Research shows," or "The data tells us," to support their claims. Being an empirical researcher and champion of quality information that dispels misinformation, I am pro–good data, studies, and research that help promote a healthier human condition. However, many of the "self-made" studies leave out or fail to discuss other factors that help people thrive outside of their own grit.

Good information helps us be objective and transforms limiting beliefs, self-defeating thoughts, and behaviors. It opens mindsets for personal and emotional growth, leading to better emotional intelligence and overall well-being. However, in the days of misinformation in social media, traditional media, marketing media, and guruism, there is a plethora of content without context.

Sometimes pertinent information and short-armed interpretations make it to the masses, resulting in misguided and unhealthy beliefs, practices, thoughts, and expectations about life and money. These can contribute to people questioning their life and money journey. They ask self-judgmental questions like, "What did I do wrong?" or comparison questions like "Why do they have what I don't?" or "What are they doing that I am not?" They might even experience jealousy: "They must have been born into money and opportunity!" These are bad for the soul. You can be a champion of hard work and mindset without the ego of "self-made."

NO ONE IS SELF-MADE!

Fans worldwide are familiar with Arnold Schwarzenegger's hard-work mindset. He is the epitome of sweat equity. If there is anyone who can claim to be self-made, "Ah-nold" has earned the right. However, Mr. Schwarzenegger finds it preposterous that someone would call themselves "self-made."[62] He's an advocate of aspirations, goal setting, action, and accountability. He also acknowledges the external contributions to developing his human capital.

He often says, "Don't call me self-made," and outright calls being self-made a myth![63,64] Mr. Schwarzenegger often says that he has had help from someone who believed in him and provided him an opportunity to build himself up. Receiving the all-important self-worth and self-value life inputs through that support gave him the confidence and the resources to focus on what brought him the most joy. This atmosphere and affirmation provided a safe space where he could commit to his aspiration fully and thus experience positive outcomes.

Of course, you need grit, commitment, courage, and consistency and must act to see results. However, without the fundamental investments of human capital of self-worth and self-value, people may be unable to fully use their action attributes. Often, when "studies show" that self-made people do not receive an inheritance, it's at the exclusion of other transferable wealth like human capital. Human capital in modern studies of humanity and economy is the investment of health, education, and training that generates talents and skills in a person that increase their productivity, making their collection of investments and skills an asset to themselves and society. It's the collective investment of human *and* financial capital across the life course, particularly in the development years, that a person can use to compound their actions, make better decisions, and practice better behaviors. They can partner these resources with their internal aspiration and drive to be self-determined instead of self-made.

THE ROLE OF LIVING GENERATIONAL WEALTH TRANSFERS IN YOUR ROAD TO TRIUMPH

Examples of in-life financial contributions that are not captured in inheritance include paid-for education expenses and expenses such as health and auto insurance, family allowing young people to stay in residence rent-free during young-adult years, and receiving life-starter funds such as down payments for homes or cars.

Other direct contributions include childcare and self-care allowances, where parents and family provide in-kind services that allow people to *directly* allocate their money, which focuses on investing in themselves. These human and financial allocation shifts help folks thrive in life and money while reducing emotional and expense tolls over time. Individuals in healthier spaces of well-being can place more energy into aspirations that they find most joyful. With less human and financial strain to overcome, these work production outcomes produce more income over time, and those inputs turn into assets and assets in to wealth.

Moreover, we cannot discount the role happenstance and luck play in our circumstances. Even Warren Buffett has said that he got a little lucky being born in the time he was, when the information gap was so wide that his studies into the stock market were more compounded then than they might have been now where information is readily available to all. Another example of good fortune is being born in the right geographic location, like a thriving country or the right ZIP codes that provide fundamental needs like safety and education. Additionally, being born into a healthy household environment with one or coupled parents gives young people additional human capital investment.

SELF-AGENCY AND SELF-ECONOMY HELP FUEL YOUR TRIUMPHS

There is power in being self-determinant and having agency over your self-economy instead of the bootstrapping grandeur and false claims of being self-made. Self-determination theory and agency theory swim in the same waters. Possessing self-determination says that every human being has three elements inside of them:

SELF-DETERMINATION ELEMENTS

Autotomy, Competence, Relatedness

Self-determination's premise is that everyone has a sense of willingly being in control of our future, wanting to master a topic, and feeling connected with a social circle or having a sense of belonging.[65]

Autonomy is the connective glue that allows you to understand your preferences and aspirations in life; competence helps you with the willing action to execute what you've learned. A sense of relatedness helps when you have compassion for your journey and a support system to continue your goals and aspirations.

Having a sense of agency helps you feel that you are in control of your journey and not place so much emphasis on the external environment.[66] A sense of agency tells you that your *inside* actions and behaviors emphasize your journey more than *outside* forces.

Two types of agencies help you make better decisions. Feeling agency is a sense of unconsciousness where you pull on embedded skill sets that have been conditioned in you and make decisions based on those already inside. Judgment agency is where we make decisions with more intent and mindfulness, thus giving us greater control. The agency gives you more control over your soundboard, producing your life keys that unlock wealth.

YOUR WHOLE SELF IS THE SOURCE OF YOUR TRIUMPHS

I believe your whole self is the source of your triumphs; this is why I led the first episodes of the LMB® Podcast with my parents. Your greatest assets are self-worth and self-value. These are assets you can build upon and that compound over time to produce value or human capital, which then produces income, and then assets, and then assets become wealth.

My parents intentionally chose to invest in self-worth, self-value, and healthy environments for me and my sister to thrive in. These inputs were and still are essential, in addition to building a holistic self. We use that holistic self to courageously believe that aspirations are possible and that we are worthy of abundance in our lives and finances if we take agency in our lives.

This is why money and emotional intelligence talk in the home, and financial socialization and self-value and self-worth building in the early stages of life are essential. Hopefully, this helps us not always to need to transform from trauma with money.

A study by The National Financial Educators Council performed in 2023 asked Americans, "During the past year, how much money do you think you lost because you lacked knowledge about personal finances?" The average answer was $1,500; about 22% said they lost at least $2,500, and almost 9% report losing $10,000 or more.[67] If you spread those average losses due to low financial education knowledge across the approximately

250 million US adults, that totals around \$388 billion.[67] A prime example of lost money and the opportunity to save and invest is the money lost to bad credit.

Have you ever truly looked at an amortization table for a mortgage loan and how much interest is paid over the life of the loan? The amount is tremendous but can be reduced with good credit. Having bad credit could move an interest rate a full 1%, costing a home buyer a quarter of a million dollars of unnecessary interest over the life of the loan and more in the missed opportunity of compounding investment returns of investing the paid interest.

Emotional reactions to the market are devastating to portfolios. Selling off in extreme downturns, trying to time the market and reentering, buying at high prices, missing out on natural recoveries after drawdowns – these all wreak havoc on long-term investment planning and could cost hundreds of thousands of dollars, if not a million or more, over time. The cost of not knowing enough about finances is staggering. And dollars do not just affect your wealth; they affect your overall aspirational well-being, your financial health, and your life health.

PRACTICE AND PASS ON GOOD MONEY HABITS

When my parents were talking about money in the home with me and my sister, they were transferring financial and life health to us that would compound over time. I'm Gen X, so allowances weren't guaranteed back in my younger days. Allowances from parents were "I allow you to eat, I allow you to sleep, I allow you to live in the house (smile!)." It was a true gift to receive frequent allowances, but it was different for each household. My parents wanted to give allowances to their children so we could have a better relationship with money and learn early the responsibilities that money requires. When we received our allowances, we had to pay ourselves first, taking 10% of our allowances and placing them inside of a general ledger book.

My mom was an accounts payable and receivable specialist at that time, so this matched her skill set, and we used an actual general ledger book. We would put 10% of our cash in the general ledger documented by line item, and our parents would match it 100%. This was our first introduction to a 401(k) matching program and the benefits of using a somewhat automated program.

In our preteen years, after paying ourselves, we had to take care of some of our personal essentials. Even though our parents had the financial means to provide for all of our needs and wants and generally did so, they wanted to instill in us that you couldn't go willy-nilly with our money once we got paid. We had to pay our future self, then begin taking care of our essentials. They made us select a few toiletries and personal care items that we would buy with our allowance – for example, toothpaste, toothbrush, and perhaps some lotion. The practice of buying essentials continued and increased when we got our first part-time jobs at 16. Early on, these life and money lessons built the foundations of money and life confidence that my sister and I still carry to this day.

UNDERSTANDING THE ROOTS OF TRIUMPH CAN TRANSFER TRIUMPH YOUR WAY

By taking a more holistic approach to building human capital through self and finances, you can take advantage of long stretches of wins in your life or be better prepared to acknowledge, admit, and act through times of trial, shortening those difficult periods, which is a triumph itself.

A holistic foundation of self-worth and self-value contributes to a constant state of gratitude. Studies show that those who live and possess higher levels of gratitude tend to make decisions and act in better behaviors that contribute to flourishing in life.[68,69] Living in a state of acknowledgment of self-determination rather than claiming to be self-made is a form of living in gratitude. It should be celebrated when individuals use a self-determination and agency mindset to help themselves thrive and, at the same time, possess gratitude for the investments that elevated their self-worth and self-value. These contributed to their success and helped them strive for their aspirational life.

Living in a state of gratitude helps the triumphant moments compound more. When you get a yes, you should celebrate it, but use gratitude for acknowledgment of the win. Then, immediately use the win to keep striving for the life you envision and the goals that are going to take you to get there.

Additionally, having a sense of gratitude can help you better process negative events. The gratitude expressed from human capital investments, possessing fortitude, and knowing that you have it in you to persevere and be resilient are far better than not having those self-worth and self-value fundamentals at all.

What Does Triumph Have to Do with Money?

Two stories come to mind of high-achieving and highly successful individuals whose early environments and installations of self-worth and self-value as social networks served as financial health transfers: Reginald Lewis and Bill Gates. These were not traditional financial generational wealth transfers in the way media, academic literature, or studies might identify because they weren't inheritances. However, human capital inputs complemented individual work ethic and ambition, leading to their extraordinary successes.

SELF-WORTH, SELF-VALUE, AND SOCIAL CAPITAL ARE COMPOUND ASSETS

Both Reginald Lewis and Bill Gates had a thirst to utilize their inherent gifts and maximize their abilities, which would ultimately achieve great amounts of wealth. Their hunger for curiosity and relentless pursuit of their aspiration, knowing what could be, and thoroughly enjoying and reveling in the rewards of the journey allowed them to bask in the awards of wealth. Essentially, they had two different paths from a socioeconomic standpoint, yet they benefited from a few common threads, and you can too!

Bill Gates grew up in the richer suburbs of Seattle, and Reginald Lewis grew up in Baltimore's tough and poor urban neighborhoods. However, both went to Harvard. Bill Gates dropped out of Harvard to continue developing the beginnings of Microsoft. Reginald Lewis went on to graduate from Harvard to conquer the world of finance through leveraged buyouts.

These two gentlemen amassed massive amounts of wealth. Gates is worth more than $100 billion from Microsoft; Lewis passed in the early 1990s at the age of 50 from brain cancer with a net worth of $400 million. Mr. Lewis and Mr. Gates have namesake foundations with legacies affecting the lives of many across the world: the Reginald F Lewis International

Law Center building at Harvard University and the Bill and Melinda Gates Foundation. What else did these two human beings have in common at the early onset of their human development?

Both have publicly stated in their books and media interviews that they are not self-made and consistently received tangible self-worth and self-value installations from parents, grandparents, loved ones, and community from early childhood and adulthood.[70,71,72] Mr. Lewis and Mr. Gates stated that these support systems, coupled with their individual high-achieving traits, their social networks in business, and higher education, were essential in their success – as was the case of Bill Gates, and his mother, Mary Gates. In fact, Mary Gates was a successful businesswoman in her own right and sat on the United Way of King County board alongside John Opal, who was then chairman of IBM. She made an introduction to Bill at a time when IBM was looking to outsource an operating system. There's a little more to that story; the rest is, as we say, history. Family systems of support and social networks matter.

CONCENTRATED INVESTMENT IN YOURSELF CAN BE LUCRATIVE

The real compoundable assets of the human condition that no one can take away can be used to produce a positive effect repeatedly, and income over life's course is your self-worth and self-value. These two assets are invaluable and priceless. You will find life and financial success if you keep investing in this two-asset portfolio.

While there is risk in concentration of investment in yourself due to forces outside your control, there are vast amounts of elements of self that you do control. If you possess certain resilient traits, matched with an unbridled drive to achieve your version of success in life and money and either a natural or developed talent, then you will have the internal answer to "bet on yourself." Taking the chance on yourself comes with great risk but can result in a great reward. The journey to concentrated triumph starts and sustains with the self-worth and self-value two-asset portfolio!

KEY TAKEAWAYS

- You can grab hold of achievement by compounding on the motivation energy from your triumphant milestone events. The act or achievement of triumph is not produced by a singular element.
- No one is self-made. Success is the collective investment of both human and financial capital across the life course that a person can use to compound their actions, make better decisions, and practice better behaviors. A person can partner these resources with their internal aspiration and drive to be self-determined instead of self-made.
- A holistic foundation of self-worth and self-value contributes to a constant state of gratitude.
- By taking a more holistic approach to building human capital through self and finances, you can take advantage of long stretches of wins in your life and shorten difficult periods, which is a triumph itself.

Journal to Find Your Financial Harmony

Feelings + Finances helps your Finances Flourish. Take time to reflect on the takeaways in this chapter. Enjoy your time and journal only what connects with you most. Any findings during your journaling discovery will help you activate the Five-Point Life Planning Process.

- What life and money themes in this chapter speak specifically to your journey?
- Can you identify opportunities in your feelings and finances to align your life and money aspirations better, giving your money assignments to achieve the life you want?
- Were there any messages in the chapter that helped you:
  - Shake social money stigmas.
  - Release or address money anxiety, judgment, or shame.
  - Move toward better security and understanding of your finances.
  - Find more contentment or fulfillment or want to find some.
  - Discover or improve your relationship with money.
- Scan the Life Money Balance® Wheel, the Six-A-Alignment System™, and the Humanity of Money™. Did content in the chapter help you see yourself in a life stage, season, preference, domain, aspiration, money goal, or mindset?

Journaling Page

CHAPTER EIGHT

ACHIEVING FINANCIAL MILESTONES

Whether in texting, social, or traditional media, you might be familiar with the plethora of acronyms and abbreviations used to communicate. There are IKR, frfr, brb, and many other short-form transmissions. Then there are the over-patterned alliterations or newly created acronyms or abbreviations to repackage common-sense ideas, attempting to refresh, reclaim, or redirect lessons or wisdom. At times, shortened communication and new acronyms are useful. Often, the not-so-long-form or original presentation is better left alone versus the modern forms that leave you wondering, *WTF*?

When it comes to your finances, there are already many barriers to starting, stopping, and sustaining. More confusion shouldn't be one of them. It would be best to have more simplicity to help you achieve your milestones. Let's find out what is useful and what is noise.

Shortened or simple frameworks that condense information help with our memory and connectivity with a subject. The use of acronyms is relatively new as the word itself was coined around 1940, and the first known English acronyms surfaced in 1879 in telegraphic code.[73]

Popular pushback is that too many acronyms can create cultural boundaries, contribute to cognitive overload leading to misinterpretation, make new people feel excluded, and make it hard to transfer information to future parties.[74] We could better explain things more simply, use our acronyms more effectively, and reserve the creation of new abbreviations and acronyms when they are most needed and efficient to deliver the most impact.

What do acronyms have to do with your wealth and well-being journey? Personal finance is filled with acronyms. To achieve or celebrate milestones, the money life journey includes many popular and applicable acronyms; still, it seems we are creating another new acronym every day.

In this chapter, we are going to start by talking about an acronym you may already know: SMART (specific, measurable, attainable, relevant, and timely) goals. As you've read this book, you know that goals are necessary building blocks to climb to reach the summit on our journey of aspiration. Aspirations are bold states of being that we strive for that nourish our fulfillment and our motivation to thrive. Goals give us measurable action steps and accountability through and toward achieving your aspirational milestones. Celebrate your milestones because they take courage, commitment, and consistency. However, moving through goals toward your aspirations is not linear.

Pathways to goals will have internal shortcomings and external interruptions along the way, which you must acknowledge, giving yourself the grace to learn and adjust for recommitment. When you have a good run of manageable life commitment and consistency, take advantage of compounding results, one building off the other and magnifying the results. Commitment and consistency also require courage, discipline, drive, and determination. Some days, this inner strength and spirit is easy to muster; other days, you must find it.

GET GOING WITH YOUR GOALS

SMART goals help you with action, accountability, adjustments, acknowledgment, and awareness. You may feel like you have heard this before. There are cries for other goal acronyms that allow for more flexibility and grace to make them more achievable and sustainable. Flexibility and grace are built into the framework. Why? Because of the inherent rewards of an aspirational journey.

Have you ever heard the stories or watched documentaries about what it takes to make a music album? The process can span weeks or many months, perhaps a year. There are the inspirations, writing, arranging, recording, producing, and multiple takes of each song on the album, with each its own goal along the way, contributing to the aspiration of making a fantastic album. Artists have often shared this story of surviving the ebbs and flows through the process. The unifying thread is the fulfillment of the process; this is the reward of their aspirational journey. The awards come on Grammy night, top album lists, People's Choice Awards, and simply release date.

Building and bridging wealth and well-being is a process. Starting and acting are the most significant moves, followed by harnessing the motivation to keep going and be sustained. Grab hold of your locus of control. Start with small goals so that the feeling of accomplishment, coupled with the measurable result, can roll over to the next, compounding the results of the journey through a snowball effect.

If I were to suggest an acronym, it would be to start SMALL: "start making actionable launches and leaps," where microevents (actionable launches) compound to larger achievements (leaps). Then, it would be best if you celebrated your milestones to fuel your courage to keep going and to tap into gratitude and fulfillment.

YOUR ASPIRATIONS AWARD THE ACHIEVEMENT AND REWARD THE JOURNEY

Aspirations are long-term.[75] To remain connected, celebrate the rewards of the process along the way. Like the aspirations they are built to fund, financial plans are also long-term. They are an integrative and collaborative roadmap to a holistic being; they require going through the Five-Point Planning Process to achieve LMB. Let's take the general timeline of being a net-worth millionaire as an example.

AVERAGE AGE FOR NET WORTH ACCUMULATION[76]

Late 30s – $500,000
Late 40s – $750,000
Around the age of 50 – $1,000,000.

More revealing is that with averages, higher outlier figures pull averages higher. In this example, the ultra-high-net-worth amounts are pulling higher averages, making people seem more on track and promoting a "not so bad" attitude. While I'm not too fond of a fearmonger, and this book encourages living your best life now *and* securing your future retirement, painting a realistic picture is helpful. Let's look at more applicable median net worths. The median number is in the middle of a large storage of numbers where 50% of the numbers are below, and the other half are above that number. For people between 50 and 59, the folks closest to retirement, the median net worth is $300,000.

Does this information contradict the notion of *and*? No. It encourages the message that *you can*! Higher net worths exist and are healthily achievable. With life and money alignment and proper assignments, celebrating milestones breeds motivation to continue the journey. The numbers also demonstrate what you *can't* do without engaging fully in your LMB. Let's look at milestones that are often misunderstood and worthy of celebrating yet often lack the permission of the inner self, society, or professionals to appreciate them fully.

We know that lifestyle creep can be detrimental to finances. As your income increases across the life course, so does unchecked subconscious or conscious spending on lifestyle goods and services at the same or higher rate. The monies allocated for lifestyle enhancement may have led to unbridled debt and low savings rates for the future, elevating anxiety and worry about the security of finances and life prospects.

In the media and personal finance expertise, lifestyle creep is generally paired with self-defeating behavior and decision-making, sudden money syndrome, and suffering from a lack of delayed gratification ability. All of this is infused with a subconscious "leveling up" of one's lifestyle, perhaps because of previous money insecurity or from maladaptive beliefs such as "keeping up with the Joneses," self-worth is net-worth, or seeking external status fulfillment. Unchecked lifestyle creep must be addressed to prevent self-destruction of finances.

There's also the concept of "disproportional materialism," a fundamental belief and value system that prioritizes material consumption to satisfy personal fulfillment and well-being. The research shows that a distorted focus and priority on material consumption contributes to high debt, low-quality relationships, bad physical health, and decreased personal well-being.[77] All of these have a high propensity to be true *if* investigations of the self, past and present, are bypassed, a pause and audit on finances are not performed, and no alignment of life and money is established.

What about a situation where well-being is *not* a flawed sense of self but an integrated investment in your quality of life (LCU, MPU, LSU) that aligns with understanding what your best life means to you – situations where your aspirations and contributions to your full self increase your ability to produce positive output and outcomes? Finding harmony does its best work when you are dispelling the shame and labels of satisfying *extrinsic* needs of "others" and empowering yourself with the permission to celebrate your *intrinsic* values and live your best life.

USE THE LMB WHEEL TO FIND THE ASPIRATIONS YOU VALUE MOST

Think of well-being as a unit of life and life as a culmination of what you value most at your stage. Visualize your LMB wheel. By understanding your past, present, and future well-being, you better understand your life units, which your increased money resources can purchase. At the stage when you experience higher incomes, what helps you live optimally with overall self-health that feeds your aspirational spirit may be to buy more near-term well-being than long-term and more material goods and services. Returning to our Average Age for Net Worth Accumulation chart, we see Generation X is a prime example of having higher income but being sandwiched between aspirations for current and future self while navigating relationships with children and elderly parents. Gen X often struggles with *balancing* their multiple aspirations. If you are Gen X, we help you unlock harmony in Chapter 11!

Lifestyle creep is a good way to celebrate your achievements within your purpose and plan. Free yourself from explaining what's best for you to others. In the same way that engaging in purchasing behavior for external affirmation from others produces adverse results, so does adhering to money social conditioning platitudes that are not in your best interest to appease external views of what financial health and life well-being are supposed to be like.

YOUR ASPIRATIONAL LIFE DOESN'T REQUIRE DEPRIVATION FRUGALITY

Financial success also requires you to get good with intentional spending habits contributing to financial health. There's a phenomenon of spending shame where a preference for frugality has swept the public's and professionals' mindsets, much of which stemmed from the popular book *The Millionaire Next Door*.[78]

The Millionaire Next Door has been successful with readers, helping provide a workable framework to approach finances through the lens of your "average" millionaire and what traits contributed to their million-dollar net worth. One of the most popular traits is being frugal by *living below your means* and not being "flashy." While the suggestion of living *below* your means is well-intentioned, it contributes to spending shame, which may keep folks from living their best life when they can afford to. An alternative approach is encouraging folks to live *within* their means, shifting them toward an intentionally aware spending success mindset. Despite potentially contributing to suboptimal well-being, preferential frugality is entrenched in personal finance education, advice, and the opinions of others.

THE DICTIONARY DEFINITIONS OF *FRUGAL*

MERRIAM-WEBSTER

1. Characterized by or reflecting economy in the use of resources
2. Careful management of material resources and especially money

http://Dictionary.com

1. Economical in use or expenditure; prudently saving or sparing; not wasteful
2. Entailing little expense; requiring few resources

http://Britannica.com

1. Careful about spending money or using things when you do not need to: using money or supplies very carefully.
2. Simple and plain

Checking with http://Thesaurus.com for synonyms of *frugal*, you will find words like *thrifty, careful, prudent, tight, penny-pinching, penny-wise,* and *miserly*. Couple these definitions with *The Millionaire Next Door*'s definition, and you can see why some folks have internal worries that they are "spending their money right" or if society or professionals with conditioned bias might suggest that they aren't "doing it right."

A few signal words of shame or restriction of well-being dollars are "simple and plain," "very careful way," "careful management," "entailing little expense," "requiring few resources," "living below your means," "penny-pinching," "tight," or "thrifty." Words and their interpretations and intent matter. These words may seem restrictive to well-being, encourage deprivation, prevent preferred choices, and label behavior as derogative with phrases such as *savings illiteracy* or *spending shame.*

Some personal finance articles attempt to soften the restricted perception of being frugal by separating it from being cheap and acknowledging the meaning of money. A recent Bankrate.com article with financial planning professionals highlights the value of spending money on quality material goods that will last, spending money on things that add value to your life, and being conscious of your dollars.[79] I regularly offer my two cents on "false frugality" with epic commentary on the *Life Money Balance Podcast.* However, these messages are not yet the norm.

SPEND SHAMING TO SPENDING SUCCESS

Let's take the stigma off intentional spending by allocating dollars to what you value most and what promotes healthy choices, moving from spending shame to spending success. For spending, discover what you value most, pay your future-self first through savings, then pay your current self by buying more units of your well-being, regardless of its form and without explanation.

Financial health is promoted by spending and savings awareness and by actions that promote current and future well-being *within,* not *below,* your means. A word like *below* suggests depriving yourself of well-being; *means* refers to something different across households, and preferences are personal. What's "flash" to someone or society, even a new luxury car, is *your* preference. And *why* you purchased your new car is unique to *you.*

The classic version of frugality, perhaps living meagerly and saving for the future at very high rates because you have an elevated future satisfaction or a muted lifestyle preference, is not a bad choice and should not be shamed. It is your preference, and so is allocating your dollars across the LMB well-being and life stage domains of LSU, LCU, and MPU. Being hungry contributes to malnutrition; you don't have to starve now to feed later. It's *and*, not *or*. If you've done all this work to identify your purpose, what's the point if you don't celebrate living your best life and hitting your milestones and goals? Find harmony and celebrate your achievements to motivate your life aspirations.

THE RETIREMENT ACRONYM SALAD

Another milestone that is often misunderstood and undercelebrated is retirement. You may have a retirement party and feel accomplished at the commencement. However, the journey and meaning of retirement have been muddied. The rewards of the achievements along the way, award of the day, and rewards of the days after take on nonsense descriptions.

Many acronyms help to explain the personal pathways to the retirement journey. There is FIRE, meaning "financial independence retire early," which is a movement of exponential current financial savings rates and sacrifices of well-being to aggressively accumulate funds to *retire early,* before the *traditional* retirement age, with some folks aspiring to retire in their 30s and 40s. There are multiple versions of FIRE.

The reason there are so many versions of FIRE is because it is just personalized retirement! Recall the acronym syndrome, where creating more acronyms can make it difficult to consistently communicate, especially when a simple explanation of an existing dynamic is more effective. Retirement is retiring *from* your *must do* to your *want to do.*

LEAN FIRE

Retiring with minimal assets to fund a minimalist retirement lifestyle.

COAST FIRE

Saving enough money to stop contributing to retirement accounts.

FAT FIRE

Aggressive funding of retirement to fund an elevated retirement lifestyle.

BARISTA FIRE

Saving enough to retire and work a part-time gig.

I know people want to shuck the old image of retirement, which seems inflexible: working 40 years to claim Social Security or start your pension at 62 at the earliest, with a retirement lifestyle and longevity determined by the available resources. This image of retirement skews the aspiration of retirement and makes accomplishing your goals to attain your retirement date less joyful.

The problem with this prescribed image is that the time you retire and how you experience retirement has always been yours to decide. Retirement has evolved, but it is *still* retirement! Consider a Cadillac or Lincoln sedan. Now, with new information, resources, and technology, you select the trimmings. Guess what? They are *still* sedans! The *what, when, where,* and *how* you retire is *personal*.

Outside of extreme external life events, retirement has always been in your control. Nowadays, retirement is more flexible and attainable, but what you do with your retirement time is yours. Retirement doesn't mean that you stop living or being productive; it means you are free of "must dos" to do your "want to dos."

To recondition retirement, I will introduce a new acronym to bring home the point. Financially retired doesn't mean finally retired.

YOUR FREEDOM STAGE

Financially Retired Embrace and Empower Doing Me (meaning you!)

Courageously aspire, envision, prepare, embark, and fund your freedom stage. During, to, and through retirement, identify your purposes and preferences, give yourself grace for adjustments, and allocate your time, well-being, and money across your life stages without apology. The financial freedom that funds and fuels your retirement journey requires the same five elements it always has. First, financial freedom is a wealth number that funds your well-being. Second, select the lifestyle you want. Third, determine how long you want to be retired. Fourth, choose your retirement date, and fifth, fund your savings rate. Using this approach, you give yourself permission to celebrate the achievements of your goals along the way and achieve your aspirations on your retirement day.

What Does Achieving Milestones Have to Do with the Money?

Many conversations equate achieving financial milestones with a money class or associating with a money culture. Misassociations and misinformation about achieving these financial milestones may contribute to false hopes, mis-alignments, and potential judgments.

Let's unpack a few common financial milestones you may hear from people and media to help you understand your life's design and wealth in the key of life as you define it. It's freeing not to be boxed in with judgments regarding your aspirations, not having to explain, living life on your own terms, and securing the confidence and clarity you need for a holistic well-being.

People love comparing themselves to others. Status is healthy in the self-actualization triangle of Maslow's Hierarchy of Needs. It can play a part in meeting intrinsic aspirations and quality of life, well-being, and social community. However, it can also be soul and financially damaging when extrinsically motivated. The number-one money rule is understanding your human and money identity – the central tenet of life and money alignment that gives your money assignment. The number-two rule is don't compare yourself to others. And if you want to know number three, you can't time the market.

DISPELLING MONEY MYTHS

To dispel money myths, promote having better relationships with money, and determine your definition of wealth and well-being, we'll discuss the money classes: middle-class, mass affluent, high net worth, and wealthy. We will exclude the uber-wealthy discussion because it's such a small subset.

Income, net worth, investable financial assets, or a combination thereof commonly define the groups. The numbers vary by source and vary by degree of age, location, and household, so I attempted to capture the gist of the categories.

HOUSEHOLD TYPE INCOME RANGE

- Middle class: $50,000 to $150,000
- Mass affluent: $150,000 to $300,000
- High Net Worth: $300,000 to $600,000
- Wealthy: $600,000 plus

HOUSEHOLD LEVELS OF RICH OR WEALTHY BY ASSET HOLDINGS[80,81]

Mass Affluent

Investable assets of $500,000 to $3 M and net worth between $500 K–$5 M, where HENRYs reside.

Truly Rich or Wealthy

Investable assets of $5–$10 million and net worth of $10–$25 million.

According to data from the *Financial Samurai* newsletter, the first level of net worth (middle class) tends to center around housing and portfolio net worth, with an index fund focus and small real estate holdings. The second level of wealth's (mass affluent) largest asset is a business, followed by an investment portfolio holding individual stocks and not owning any index funds, a primary residence, and multiple real estate investments.[82] Both of these groups intentionally and mindfully spend money on their lifestyle well-being preferences without apology, with data showing that they avoid spending money on cheaply made products, instead paying for more quality goods and services that last longer and increase well-being, including entertainment, travel, clothing, home goods, domestic services, and automobiles.[83,84]

I often hear folks express frustration about where they *should be*, how they *should be* living, and what they don't have. They may express frustration about what they *could be* having or what they *should be* investing in based on

---

UNDERSTANDING GROUPS TO HELP MONEY CONFIDENCE

1. Better understand your internal financial milestone journeys and where your comfort levels are.

2. Develop realistic risk and investment mindsets.

3. Investigate what LMB domains and facets you want to address on your terms.

---

what someone else is investing in. Worse yet, they may compare their financial plan to someone else's without knowing other folks' aspirations and life journeys. All these *shoulds* and *coulds* drive home the idea that personal finances are personal and that financial life planning is about your life.

GOING ABOUT BUILDING WEALTH

Progress with your life and finances is not rewarded with complexity. You will achieve money life milestones with commitment, consistency, and compounding. Surprise! Here comes another acronym: KISS. Jokingly, but seriously, it means "keep it simple, stupid!" When clients at Concurrent Financial Planning have asked me over the years what's next in their investment portfolio as they achieve higher levels of income and net worth, often, the answer is "more of the same." On the wealth side, the next question that gives the most utility is, "How are you going to use your new levels of wealth to fund your keys of life?"

Becoming wealthy in a manner that supports your well-being in the way that you define it is what matters most. The formula is income to assets, assets to wealth, and wealth to fund your well-being. Focus less on whether you are a W-2 professional or an entrepreneur. Focus more on consistency, commitment, and concentration surrounded by diversification, increasing multiple streams of income, and appreciating assets. The strategies to accumulate wealth are endless.

WAYS TO BUILD WEALTH

1. Increase income by consistently negotiating higher salaries, becoming more skilled at your craft and more valuable to your firm.

2. Potentially transfer to another firm or port out of your firm after years of service to transfer your built-up skill set to start a practice.

3. Demand equity compensation or bonuses along with your income.

4. Participate in your employee stock purchase plan and contribute to your tax-deferred retirement plans to receive matches.

5. Include cash flow investment real estate properties, individual or commercial, starting with one and then two.

6. Start hobby side hustles that increase income by supplementing your main income.

7. If you have the grit and determination, all-out invest in your will to succeed and invest in your business for three to seven years, and when your business becomes successful, use those income streams to diversify your business by investing in the financial markets.

THE CONFLICTION OF BUSINESS CONCENTRATION RISK SUCCESS

You'll hear books, media, and financial gurus often misjudge or misconstrue concentration risk. Yes, you can build large sums of wealth of concentration in a single business or single stocks or many other things; often underreported are the associated risks with overconcentration.

What's more ideal is strategic concentration, or understanding the concentration risks before you enter. Of course, everyone has their own appetite for risk or capacity to take risk. All said, one of this book's central themes is preferences and maximizing personal utility. Select the aspirational profession that's best for you and your household that will bring you joy and the best economic prospects, and maximize it to the best of your ability. Don't let glamorized, saturated, and often parroted information cloaked as advice steer you in a wealth and well-being direction that is not your path.

One common statistic you'll hear about becoming a millionaire is that almost 90% of millionaires own businesses. That may be true, but what is not reported often enough is that 50% of businesses fail in the first year, 20% fail within 2 years, and 65% within 10 years.[85] Many fail through lack of funding. Only 10% of startups are successful,[85] and about 50% of business owners report high stress levels.[86]

Survivor bias dominates success stories, and as we've discussed, the term *self-made* is very misleading. Becoming a business owner is high risk and reward, mostly based on your intrinsic *why*, and inherent purpose-based factors are commonly left unexplained in these statistics.

BE CONFIDENT IN YOUR WEALTH BUILDING

Frankly, there is no get-rich-quick scheme. Sure, if your business survives and thrives on average, you could quicken the time you could become a millionaire compared to being a corporate professional. That said, your corporate professional journey could bode well for you and compound your wealth greatly. Either way, you are talking about a timeline of 15–30 years, more likely

20–30 years. Other predictors of millionaire success include higher education, specifically college education, commitment and consistency to your craft whether W-2 professional or entrepreneur, and optimal life and financial decisions over time that are allowed to compound without interruption.

That compounding without interruption is a huge unknown, and no one is immune to the uncertainties of life. This is where the no shame, no judgment, grace, grit, and gratitude come into play. You simply don't know someone else's life, and you must work through yours with better understanding and allow for adjustments to a process that allows you to navigate life and money more healthily.

KEY TAKEAWAYS

- When it comes to your finances, there are already many barriers to starting, stopping, and sustaining. More confusion shouldn't be one of them. It would be best to have more simplicity to help you achieve your milestones.
- Misassociations and misinformation about achieving financial milestones may contribute to false hopes, misalignments, and potential judgments.
- Another milestone that is often misunderstood and undercelebrated is retirement. Outside of extreme external life events, retirement has always been in your control.
- Progress with your life and finances is not rewarded with complexity. You will achieve money life milestones with commitment, consistency, and compounding.

Journal to Find Your Financial Harmony

Feelings + Finances helps your Finances Flourish. Take time to reflect on the takeaways in this chapter. Enjoy your time and journal only what connects with you most. Any findings during your journaling discovery will help you activate the Five-Point Life Planning Process.

- What life and money themes in this chapter speak specifically to your journey?
- Can you identify opportunities in your feelings and finances to align your life and money aspirations better, giving your money assignments to achieve the life you want?
- Were there any messages in the chapter that helped you:
  - Shake social money stigmas.
  - Release or address money anxiety, judgment, or shame.
  - Move toward better security and understanding of your finances.
  - Find more contentment or fulfillment or want to find some.
  - Discover or improve your relationship with money.
- Scan the Life Money Balance® Wheel, the Six-A-Alignment System™, and the Humanity of Money™. Did content in the chapter help you see yourself in a life stage, season, preference, domain, aspiration, money goal, or mindset?

Journaling Page

_____

_____

_____

_____

_____

_____

_____

_____

_____

_____

_____

_____

_____

_____

_____

CHAPTER NINE

TRANSITIONING WITH WILLING TRANSFORMA- TION

My childhood was full of the best cartoons ever made! The top-rated 1980s and 1990s children's cartoon *Voltron: Defender of the Universe* captures the essence of transformation and transition to the next stage in your LMB journey. The show's backdrop is the Voltron Force, which comes together through the formation of five robot lions commanded by space pilots to protect Planet Arus from evil forces from Planet Doom.[86] The individual lions integrate their unique strengths, transforming from singular units to a unified force and using their special powers to take on challenges and emerge victorious!

The moment after you've been through the beginning phases of the stages of change reflected in the Six-A Financial Harmony System – you admit where you are and acknowledge how you feel so you can take action – the transform and transition part of aligning, aspiring, and achieving your aspirations is the most fun! Life's transition following transformation requires you to embrace your current life stage, your ideal self, and the life you envision.

THE VOLTRON LIONS[87] AND THE VICTORY OF YOUR JOURNEY

When the Voltron Lions came together, it was a moment of empowerment to take on all comers, a sign of strength, hope, and overall health and well-being using integrated states to become a whole unit. The fascinating part is that a human piloted each lion – just like you power your money journey.

Each part of the Voltron robot – the red, black, yellow, blue, and green lions – had special powers. Voltron's greatest strength was intentional consciousness possessing awareness, courage, and willingness to fight the good fight. These attributes can be applied to your LMB journey.

The Black Lion was the head and could create a shield, a great representation of a mindset possessing the ability to process adversity and attack limiting beliefs. The Black Lion sums up the bravery to be empowered, abundantly applying all of the resources toward the goals at hand. The Red Lion was the right hand. Its capability was a blazing sword and a cannon with the firepower to home in on the target and blast away.

The Green Lion was the left arm, and its ability was to be flexible and adaptive, which allowed integration of the Lions, making it more interchangeable and empowering the sum of its parts. The Blue Lion was the right leg, had freezing capabilities, and possessed good sensory mechanisms. In our money life, the special powers of the Green and Blue Voltron Lions can be used for heightened awareness, mindfulness reflection, and motivation, sensing the times across life to take an honest self-audit to advance our journey. Having the power to freeze a moment in time allows for analysis, pausing to figure out where you are now and where you want to go.

The Yellow Lion is on the left leg and has another cannon; its special power is defense. On your LMB journey, having a moat around your life and finances and blinders around your eyes is essential to keep you looking forward and focused on your journey and not on the journeys of others. The Yellow Lion moves faster than light. When you are transforming to align your current self with your ideal self and transitioning to the next stage, you want to move full speed ahead! Possessing good defense allows you to have resilience and not relapse into old ways during and after adversity, giving you more power to roll and adapt during those times and fall forward rather than fall.

When all the Voltron Lions unite to protect the planet – when your current and ideal self come together – you are more empowered to shake off perceptions of others and past perceptions of yourself and society. The pieces of Voltron coming together are like all the music notes, and you can bring them together to arrange your song with the keys of life and money, bridging wealth and well-being to find harmony.

TRANSFORMING YOUR LIFE AND MONEY WITH POSITIVE PSYCHOLOGY

Permission and positivity help you transform and transition your money life. When I mention positivity, I'm not suggesting toxic positivity, which suggests that just thinking positively will solve everything.

There are situations and stages of life where the only positivity you can call on that day is "six and two" which is six feet above ground and two feet on.

In the days and ages of social media, *reel* life and *real* life are different. Many folks are projecting a false front of positivity. Comparing your journey with others is fruitless because it's impossible to know the stories, paths, and preferences of others. Having the courage to wake up and navigate life the best you can that day is a win. Positivity is an abundant mindset, but a mindset alone won't achieve prosperity. Positivity has additional components as well.

THE PERMA MODEL OF POSITIVE PSYCHOLOGY AND YOUR FINANCES

In 2011, Dr. Martin Schlageman developed The PERMA model of positive psychology. PERMA has five elements: positive emotion, engagement, relationships, meaning, and achievement.[88,89] He thought these were essential to achieve a healthy sense of overall well-being.

Through a financial therapy lens, bridging personal finance philosophies and practices with the psychology aspects, the research outcome suggests that those who embody the elements of PERMA have healthier finances, better overall well-being, and self-efficacy (which is a more positive outlook on future aspects of well-being and finances).[90] Applying the PERMA model to your life and money journey helps your finances flourish. You are evoking these pillars in your money life to have them work together, empowering you to live the life you want.

POSITIVE EMOTION

Positive emotions mean thinking positively for positive outcomes and not necessarily thinking positively for positivity's sake or projecting fake positive emotions. Having an uplifting outlook with the belief that things can and will get better helps you maintain an abundant mindset. Thinking positively doesn't guarantee positive results. However, when you do not attempt a positive outlook, you have less chance of thriving the way you want. This thought process concerns the internal locus of control and the belief that you can produce the life you want.

ENGAGEMENT

Engagement is about being in a state of flow – being surrounded by work and productivity in a deeply fulfilling way. Being engaged continuously also contributes to overall happiness; understanding what brings you happiness ultimately saves you money because you're not using your money to fill a void.

RELATIONSHIPS

Relationships are essential to have with loved ones, friends, family, and even people in your profession. People naturally want to relate to other human beings. One of the reasons why people spend so long in their professions is that it's hard to transition to the next thing because of the relationships they have forged. Like an investment portfolio, think long-term and grab hold of relationships that can last.

Your relationships are going to uplift you through tough times and embolden the great times. Furthermore, you'll find that some of your dollars will be invested in being connected with your social circle, and in that social circle will be the higher levels of self-actualization – esteem, status, love, and affection – all of which are important to reach a higher sense of self.

MEANING

The next element of the PERMA model is meaning, which immensely contributes to your purpose. In the 5ix A Financial Harmony System, knowing what you value most in the life stage that you are in helps you establish life and money alignment, giving assignments to your dollars. Here we are again at your connective glue, determining and funding your *why* and what brings you joy.

Lastly, folks want to feel a sense of accomplishment, highlighting the importance of goals within aspirations. What is an aspiration if you can't reach it? What is an aspiration if you feel that you're not advancing toward it? This is another area in Maslow's triangle where wants are needs too! Achieving aspirational wants helps you live in a higher state of well-being. The feelings you get from accomplishments are more glue that sticks you to your plan and purpose. More accomplishments serve as more motivation to realize those feelings.

To experience a transformational change, you must firmly believe it's the change you want and that you can maintain your change. You must also permit yourself to transition to the life you want. Remember that everyone's journey is their own; when you transform and transition to your state of change, everyone can't come with you. Your job is not to encourage them to embark on their own journey; they must do that themselves. You can live a life of testimony that people can witness and ask you what you are doing because they want some of that too!

What Does Transformation Have to Do with the Money?

I want to keep the focus on your journey. Central to the reason why I do what I do, and the reason why I'm impacting lives by advancing the human condition of others through financial advice, is story and testimony. My testimony comes from transformation, and I hope picking up my story helps you get where you want to go.

Transformation takes courage and consistency. You must have stick-to-itiveness for 12 months – 6 months in the action stage and 6 months in the maintenance stage. You may ask, "What does transformation mean? What does the process of financial planning mean? What does the Humanity of Money mean? What does *it* all mean?" I recall an answer I received while talking with my grandfather when I was 13. After telling me his life story, he asked me, "Do you understand what I'm saying to you, son?" and I said, "A little bit, Grandfather, but not really." He responded, "Just keep living, son, just keep living."

What I'm saying here is that you don't know what *it* is until you've gone through some *it*! You can place a *sh* before that last *it* if you like. Life will life. Transformation in life and money is a beautiful achievement coming from where you've been and going where you want to go.

SECURE YOUR BAG!

The phrase "secure the bag" has an urban dictionary meaning of getting money or accomplishing your goal, sometimes used in slang, perhaps finding its origin in Hip-Hop songs.[91] From a person who was bagging on acronyms in the previous chapter (pun intended), I view securing the bag differently, with *bag* meaning "Be a G" – "G" meaning grace and gratitude. *Be a person who has grace and gratitude in your life's pursuit, purpose, and prosperity!*

When you secure your bag in this way, you have worked your way through the Six-A Financial Harmony System and experienced real change with your life and money. This is life aspiration, where wealth is buying more units of your well-being, true financial harmony – the very definition of *Wealth in the Key of Life*.

MY LMB TESTIMONY TO HELP INSPIRE YOUR JOURNEY

People have asked me why I haven't written a book for the last couple of years and shared my wisdom and guidance with the world. Even my own father has said, "Son, the world is waiting on you." Other peers and colleagues have said, "Where is your book?" Aside from being extremely busy making an impact with the gifts God gave me, folks thought I was procrastinating on the book, which was a signal of a limiting belief. The truth is I started writing this book to you during my transformation in 2016. After the grueling Honest Self-Audit stage of admitting, acknowledging, acting, aligning, aspiring, and achieving, I began living my aspirations and creating my life design right then and there.

In 2016, I began to reshape my life when I got accepted into the doctoral Personal Financial Planning program at Texas Tech University. When I walked into the halls of Texas Tech and a temporary pause from a professional career back into academia, I ran into one of my mentors, Deena Katz. She saw me in the hallways, immediately called me into her office, and asked me, "What the hell are you doing back on campus when you should be thriving in the professional world?"

I shared with her my story, what I'd been through, what my plan was, and how being there would help me achieve my purpose. I wanted to advance the human condition through financial advice, combining academia, a financial advisor firm, public speaking, teaching, authorship, entertainment, and education. All of it! She said, "Okay, you can stay!"

This is the type of transformation I aim to give to you and to others and what has inspired the LMB philosophy. I hope my story helps answer the *it* question and the question of "What does that have to do with the money?" at the end of each chapter. It has everything to do with money!

You see, everything that has been placed into me from my parents, my family, my sister, brother-in-law, niece, first mentor Dr. Jan Jasper, close friends, my wife, my reasons for seasons, values, experiences, attitudes culture – that is the identity, the purpose. It took continuous understanding to unlock the "why" to shape that into purpose, placing that into a financial plan with alignment, giving my money assignments. My *Wealth in the Key of Life* is a classic song that everyone can listen to, that can touch their spirit – and I can listen to yours so yours can touch mine.

KEY TAKEAWAYS

- The moment after you've been through the beginning phases of the stages of change reflected in the Six-A Financial Harmony System, the transform and transition part of aligning, aspiring, and achieving your aspirations is the most fun!
- Permission and positivity help you transform and transition your money life. Having positive emotions means thinking positively for positive outcomes and not necessarily thinking positively for positivity's sake or projecting fake positive emotions.
- It is essential to know that once you experience a transformational change, you can maintain your change because it is the change that you want. You must permit yourself to transition to the life you want.

Journal to Find Your Financial Harmony

Feelings + Finances helps your Finances Flourish. Take time to reflect on the takeaways in this chapter. Enjoy your time and journal only what connects with you most. Any findings during your journaling discovery will help you activate the Five-Point Life Planning Process.

- What life and money themes in this chapter speak specifically to your journey?
- Can you identify opportunities in your feelings and finances to align your life and money aspirations better, giving your money assignments to achieve the life you want?
- Were there any messages in the chapter that helped you:
  - Shake social money stigmas.
  - Release or address money anxiety, judgment, or shame.
  - Move toward better security and understanding of your finances.
  - Find more contentment or fulfillment or want to find some.
  - Discover or improve your relationship with money.
- Scan the Life Money Balance® Wheel, the Six-A-Alignment System™, and the Humanity of Money™. Did content in the chapter help you see yourself in a life stage, season, preference, domain, aspiration, money goal, or mindset?

Journaling Page

_____

_____

_____

_____

_____

_____

_____

_____

_____

_____

_____

_____

_____

_____

_____

_____

_____

CHAPTER TEN

FINANCIAL PLANNING FOR A FULFILLING LIFE

F inancial wellness is a public good and we are all deserving of it. The LMB philosophy, using the Six-A Financial Harmony System, allows you to navigate the Arc of Financial Wellness. Life and money are unified journeys beginning with your unique self and the quest to link your current self with your ideal self. It can be hard to grasp the notion that your current self and your future self are the same self.

> ## THE ARC OF FINANCIAL WELLNESS™
>
> Financial Compassion, Financial Education, Financial Literacy, Financial Wellness.

FINANCIAL COMPASSION

Financial compassion is the mix of the unique ingredients that make up your attitudes, experiences, cultures, values, and preferences about money, the life you've lived through to now, and the life you want to live. Compassion is about the courageous vulnerability to explore and understand where you are, and want to go, and tapping into your willingness and capacity to do something about it. Compassion is all about the HSA within the Six-A Financial Harmony System.

FINANCIAL EDUCATION

When you feel understood, financial education and recommendations you learn or receive from your trusted sources and professionals begin to click because once you open the heart, you open the mind. The heart and mind are in a healthier state to receive information and suggestions, in this case, in the form of financial education that will help you strive forward and thrive.

FINANCIAL LITERACY

Then comes financial literacy, which is *understanding* your life and money to make *informed* decisions and engage in behaviors that will put you in a position to prosper. The key to financial literacy is being informed. You may find pushback on financial literacy because the connotation may lead to shame and judgment by implying illiteracy; that's why the Arc of Financial Wellness begins with compassion.

You must understand the unique situation and self where you can be affirmed, heard, and belong. Secondly, like financial wellness, overall financial literacy is needed across *all* socioeconomic statuses, including the well-off. Education and being informed to make better decisions and engage in more productive behaviors apply to *all* life journeys. However, all life journeys exist in different places and require different applications.

FINANCIAL WELLNESS

This brings us to financial wellness, which is the ability to manage your finances to obtain more confidence and clarity, making you feel more secure about your finances and life prospects. When you feel holistically well, you can feel financially well. And being financially well helps fund your aspirations. Financial planning strategies, even the most complex, get easier to define and deliver when you control and connect your finances to your story.

MONEY IS MORE THAN A TOOL; IT'S A PARTNER

When we say money is just a tool to live, it sounds about right, but the soul of money is missing from that statement, and the role money plays in our lives is discounted. A tool is a device that is used to carry out a certain action. A popular cliche is that we have "tools in our toolbox," and money is one of those tools that we use to carry out the meaning of life – such as our *why* or our life's purpose, making life "more than money."

Just like the domains of financial planning are integrated across life's course, the domains and life stages of the LMB are integrated, and so too are your life and money. Life and money are partners. If we can commonly use the word *tool* to help explain money's role in our lives, we can also use *partner*. The definition of a partner is to be associated with one another in action, to serve as a couple in an intimate relationship, or as two persons who dance together.

How applicable that image is when you are thinking about two souls representing the Humanity of Money, coming together where money is part of our existence and our self-economy and dancing to the music of the keys of life, bridging wealth and well-being. It's okay to think about money differently and shake the stigmas of society, making it less taboo and embracing your relationship with money because money has a relationship with you.

You have the permission, and you are worthy to want more until you have more than enough! In both instances, you are worthy to live abundantly in your money and your life pursuits. You want more of what you understand as happiness because you've done the work understanding your past, present, and future, determining what you don't want to do and what you do want to do.

YOUR FINANCIAL PLAN IS YOUR LIFE PLAN

Financial planning is life planning, life-centered planning, or, put another way, lifestyle financial planning. The terms and process of *life planning* or *life-centered planning* were introduced by George Kinder and Mitch Anthony, respectively. The approach proposes to move financial planning from an asset focus to a life focus, centered around life stories that fuel the finances of planning. The approach moves beyond return on investments (ROI) with an ultimate goal of return on life (ROL).

Before being introduced to life planning, my story and experiences, coupled with my professional practices, led to the development of LMB – *let your life lead your money.* So, after continually pouring into the philosophy with additional insights from other frameworks – financial psychology, continued professional practices, theory, and the application to clients' lives – the LMB or Integrated Life well-being approach gained depth and continues to help people find financial harmony.

Frankly, there's a genius to the original process of financial planning that always had and has life planning, financial psychology, financial advice, identity, and stories, past, present, and future embedded in the journey – all the ingredients together make financial planning powerful. The art of collaborative financial planning between you and the planner is the delivery, environment, encouragement, and empowerment mechanics by the professional and your belief, engagement, action, and resilience. Match the art with the science of meaningful and measurable financial strategies and you have life and money magic!

THE ALCHEMIST IS THE BEST PERSONAL FINANCE BOOK!

There are several books I've read in my life that continue to have a profound impact. I'm certain you have yours, and hopefully, *WIKL* will make your shelf of guideposts for your journey. One book I have read across multiple life stages is *The Alchemist*.[92] Like the LMB, *The Alchemist* points out that each life stage matters, and each distinct life stage requires meaning and understanding. The first few pages of *The Alchemist* are riveting, grabbing your soul from the jump. The book follows Santiago's bold and courageous journey to better understand his meaning of life and value system, discover his aspirations, and learn how he's going to achieve the life he wants. Soaking up information and wisdom along the way, he examines his internal self and accepts education through information and the wisdom of others, what Santiago calls "a search for a personal calling."

My parents raised me and my sister to be humanists and have a willingness to learn about the unique experiences, cultures, and attitudes of people, which helps us grow through knowing our place in the world, a form of humility. One of those areas is having a spiritual faith, and every person's spiritual faith in God – how they define God – is their personal relationship, which makes the words and the first few pages of *The Alchemist* so profound.

"A personal calling is God's blessing. It is the path that God chose for you here on Earth. Whenever we do something that fills us with enthusiasm We are following our legend. However, we don't all have the courage to confront our own dream."(p. x)

The book goes on to explain that to grab hold of your abundant life you must overcome four obstacles.

1. Overcome the fear of the impossible, which can be transcribed as limiting beliefs and inaction toward the life we value most – our personal calling, a deep, burning desire.
2. Possess the courage to pursue this dream with the love of ourselves and the love of those around us who will be a part of our life story.
3. Have the courage to overcome fears and failures. Be vulnerable in a way that allows you to explore where you are, to better understand and utilize your failures and investigations. Use these lessons to build greater confidence and resilience in the pursuit of your aspirational life and keep fighting the good fight.
4. Possess the audacity to strive for and *live* the life of your dreams.

Throughout the book, Santiago explores his personal legend. Your personal legend is your statement of financial purpose, coming together with your financial statements, to help build your aspirational life and tell your story. As we've discussed, when you tap into your story, you tap into your money.

The Alchemist has been translated into more than 50 languages and published in countries across the world, selling over 50 million copies. Tongue in cheek, I hope my book sells the same because that means that people all over the world have embraced a new program and a new normal of their relationship with money, better understanding the partnership of life and money. It would mean they are permitting themselves to partner their wealth and well-being to forge through and to their aspirational life, accepting their worthiness to live abundantly and affirming the courage it takes to survive and thrive in the life they envision.

The LMB philosophy using the Six-A Financial Harmony System and the Five-Point Planning Process provide you a framework and a guidepost to build and bridge your life and money to find harmony. At every stage of the system, there are economic, financial, and psychological theories, evidence, and experienced-based practicalities that make what you are going through and going to do better understood, accepted, and normalized.

Hopefully, this affirmation will give you the energy and motivation to get where you want to go and enjoy that place when you arrive. Think of the LMB philosophy as swim lessons to help you swim through the Sea of C's in financial planning, which are confidence, clarity, control, and conversation, to explore with yourself and others such as your family, spouse, cross-generations, and friends. These conversations help you explore the *why* and meaning of your money and life's course. The keys of life are yours!

COLLABORATE WITH COMPREHENSIVE FINANCIAL PLANNING

The process of financial planning includes working with a certified financial planning professional who adheres to a fiduciary standard and works collaboratively, integrating relevant elements of your finances and your current and future life with you to help you achieve your life and money goals. They should communicate transparent fees and services. You might ask, what is that *F* word? And no, it's not a curse word.

WHAT IS A FIDUCIARY?

A financial planner professional who holds a CFP® certification that promises *to act in your best interest at all times.*

A Statista report published in 2024 showed that in 2022, only 35% of Americans used a financial advisor.[93] A similar study by Edelman Financial Engines was conducted in 2022 to study affluent households with assets ranging from $500,000 to $3 million; 35% of households had a financial advisor.[94] An underwhelming number of households in America are using a financial advisor, which is concerning because those who use an advisor consistently report that they are less stressed and more confident in their life and money prospects now and for retirement.

For example, in the Edelman Report, of those who did not work with a financial professional, 52% reported feeling stressed about their money, compared to only 39% feeling stressed when working with a professional.[94] Continuing with the Edelman report among the affluent and among Americans overall, the biggest barrier to working with a financial professional is the perceived cost of advice.[94]

THE COST OF FINANCIAL ADVICE

You may have heard that most financial advisors charge a 1% fee for their services. That 1% fee gets all the news and is hotly contested in places like

Reddit. This chapter is not here to sell you on services; this book is about your overall wealth and well-being. I want you to have clear information when you are considering your financial planning journey, whether or not you choose to work with a financial planning professional.

First, that 1% fee, in the historical context, used to be for investments only, meaning a financial advisor used to charge you 1% to manage your portfolio and offer you no other services. They sold you mutual funds or stocks with more fees, then set it and forgot it, placing it on autopilot. They collected a fee from you, leaving you feeling underserved and with a lack of connection to your overall life goals. This was the industry norm for financial advisors for a long time.

FINANCIAL PLANNING ADVICE IS COMPREHENSIVE

That has changed now. All financial planners are financial advisors, but not all financial advisors are financial planners. The profession and process of financial planning consists of many relevant personal finance domains:[95]

- Education planning
- Cash flow management
- Risk management and insurance planning
- Employee benefits
- Retirement and income planning
- Estate planning
- Tax planning
- Investment planning
- Psychology of financial planning (and more)

These domains are integrated, meaning the decisions of multiple domains affect the others, and the actions and outcomes happen across life's course – which makes financial planning comprehensive. Planning is connective, matching people with a process that aligns their life and finances. The process is personal with a purpose and delivers a plan that includes values, experiences, attitudes, and culture. Comprehensive financial planning is your ideal financial advice experience. For this you pay 1% of your assets under management or a flat financial advice fee. It's key to remember that you're paying for the *comprehensive* financial advice, the financial planning relationship, and the effect of the outcomes the advice and relationship have on your life and finances across your journey – the *value* you are receiving from the advice.

DECIDING YOUR GOOD FIT FOR SERVICE AND FEES – IT'S ABOUT THE VALUE AND QUALITY OF ADVICE

People tend to want more control over where their fee payment comes from – fee account location. The fee can be an annual asset under management fee paid quarterly from their investment portfolio, a money market or checking account, or an annually paid quarterly flat fee paid from an investment portfolio, money market, or checking account, or it can be a one-time upfront financial advice fee, which is attractive to do-it-yourself investors.

Some pushback comes from the public that when the investment portfolio gains wealth, the variable AUM (assets under management) fee increases, and that standpoint is valid. That said, household finances may or may not have become more complex. The market doesn't go up every year; however, the service received is valuable every year. That said, a flat fee or advice fee may be more applicable and may not increase at the rate that a variable AUM does over time. Conversely, like with everything else, inflation will eventually affect your flat fee financial planning prices and so these will also go up over time.

FINDING YOUR IDEAL FINANCIAL ADVICE RELATIONSHIP

How much you pay in fees is about the value of the financial advice you feel you are receiving. If you find significant value in the services, then you will view your fee as an investment in your comprehensive wealth and well-being. There's no wrong fee here, only the one that's right for you.

Three of the key components of a financial planning relationship are the relationship itself, the complexity of the finances, and time. It's of note that anyone can invest vast amounts of time to become an expert at anything, but effective planning of your finances requires an extensive investment of time. Even if someone chooses not to become an expert choosing to put in the time, are they okay with the efficiency of the time spent or the quality of their results? Time and expertise are hard to spend, build, or come by.

I'll leave you with more information that you may find valuable for your financial professional collaboration consideration. JD Power conducts an annual study about what folks value most about a financial advisor's relationships and what they view as ideal financial advice:[96]

PEOPLE WANT IDEAL FINANCIAL ADVICE

1. Does the relationship deliver a comprehensive financial plan?

2. Does the advisor ensure that the client fully understands the fees that they pay?

3. Does the financial planner have an integral part in the client's life?

4. Does the financial planner have an intimate understanding of the client's lifestyle?

5. Does the financial planner place the client's best interest first?

Software giant e-Money suggests that people value advisor knowledge, trust, transparency of fees, and a financial planning thought leader.[97] The American College of Financial Planning suggests that people value advisor knowledge and trustworthiness, and advisors who can understand goals and communicate financial concepts.[98]

PEOPLE WHO COLLABORATE WITH IDEAL ADVICE ARE THRIVING

As you can see, there are a lot of common threads here, and you may see many deliverables and services that you value most in the planners that you would like to collaborate with. When considering collaborating with a financial planner, I want you to have this information with you. Unfortunately, when it comes to the ideal financial advice experience described in the JD Power data, only 11% of people receive that type of advice from their advisor.[96,99]

Here's another little nugget for those of you in higher income and wealth brackets. Fidelity reports that among the millionaire and decamillionaire clients they surveyed at their firm, 22% and 82% said they have a *trusted* relationship with an financial advisor.[100] What is that data saying? Folks who are thriving are curious about their financial lives now and later want more confidence, value their time, want to be informed, and appreciate the collaboration with a beneficial planner-client relationship.[99] Once better understood, they want to see their money life aspirations come to fruition so they can handle life's ebbs and flows across their life course, and you don't have to be a millionaire. Dandy if you are and dandy if you are on your way! It's about the journey and how you maximize your mindset, decisions, emotions, finances, and aspirations. Also, trusted professional services that are meaningful and measurable wouldn't hurt.

When building your wealth and well-being, I'd rather you not be overwhelmed, underprepared, and oversold when working with a professional. Let's close the show with the music that you want to hear: LMB represents life's continuum, and the previous nine chapters of this book represent life's continual course and the integration of your life and money in your life's continual progress.

What Does Financial Planning Have to Do with the Money?

Snoop Dogg was onto something back in the day when he said, "I've got my mind on my money and my money on my mind." Who knew that rap lyrics would associate so well with the LMB Journey and the global Humanity of Money?

There are large segments of people who, while they have money on their mind, say that personal finance books like these are too generic, that they don't apply to them, that they say nothing new, what was the point? That's why this book keeps addressing the question, "What does that have to do with the money?" The answer each time is "everything." Each time, that "everything" applies to a different element of LMB. How so?

PEOPLE ARE SEARCHING FOR TRUSTED SOURCES AND SERVICES

Many folks read books like these and find their journey as they turn the pages. You find gems of information all from one book that really resonates with you or a few of them across many books that culminate in one guiding life and money value system.

Others read a few books that don't speak to them and then finally find one from someone they resonate with. The information speaks directly to their journey and informs where they've been, where they are, and where they want to go. Because money is essential to existence, they search for answers from trusted resources or advisors that resonate with them and then advocate for that resource because they want others to feel the same way.

They leave reviews on their favorite bookstore or website, they share on social media, they give the books as gifts, talk about it in their conversations, you get the gist. People are seeking answers for a holistic approach to finding harmony between wealth and well-being and a better understanding of how they partner. I grew up in Houston, Texas, and they used to call the Astrodome the Eighth Wonder of the World. I'm beginning to believe that personal finances, wherever you are in your journey, have made the Wonders of the World lists.

So, what about those folks who say books like these don't apply to higher-income or wealthy people or to people with better self-proclaimed financial literacy; is this book just one in a batch of many? First, if you made it this far, I hope that's not the case. We've chopped it up through these chapters on wealth, and the keys of life with a different lens and viewpoints that I hope help you process your journey with the permission and information to get you where you want to go, to the life the way you define it.

KEY TAKEAWAYS

- Financial wellness is a public good and we are all deserving of it. The LMB philosophy, using the Six-A Financial Harmony System, allows you to navigate the Arc of Financial Wellness, linking your current self with your ideal self.
- Financial compassion is about the courageous vulnerability to explore and understand where you are, and want to go, and tapping into your willingness and capacity to do something about it.
- Money is more than a tool. It's a partner.
- *The Alchemist* – the best personal finance book – points out that life stage matters where each unique life stage requires meaning and understanding.
- The process of financial planning includes working with a certified financial planning professional who adheres to a fiduciary standard and works a collaborative process, integrating relevant elements of your finances and your current and future life with you to help you achieve your life and money goals.
- One study reports that about 80% of higher-income households collaborate with a financial advisor. People are thriving collaborating with financial planning professionals.

Journal to Find Your Financial Harmony

Feelings + Finances helps your Finances Flourish. Take time to reflect on the takeaways in this chapter. Enjoy your time and journal only what connects with you most. Any findings during your journaling discovery will help you activate the Five-Point Life Planning Process.

- What life and money themes in this chapter speak specifically to your journey?
- Can you identify opportunities in your feelings and finances to align your life and money aspirations better, giving your money assignments to achieve the life you want?
- Were there any messages in the chapter that helped you:
  - Shake social money stigmas.
  - Release or address money anxiety, judgment, or shame.
  - Move toward better security and understanding of your finances.
  - Find more contentment or fulfillment or want to find some.
  - Discover or improve your relationship with money.
- Scan the Life Money Balance® Wheel, the Six-A-Alignment System™, and the Humanity of Money™. Did content in the chapter help you see yourself in a life stage, season, preference, domain, aspiration, money goal, or mindset?

Journaling Page

CHAPTER ELEVEN

GENERATION X CAN HELP UNLOCK FINANCIAL HARMONY

One driving force of this book is to think differently about money. By looking through the lens of the Humanity of Money and developing a better understanding, alignment, and assignment using LMB, hopefully, you can change how you relate to and prosper with money. Right now, one generation most notably captures the cross-generational transition in how they and their families handle life and money: Generation X (Gen X).

Money is cross-generational, and Gen X captures multiple generations at once. Having been influenced by their elders emotionally and financially, Gen X is, in turn, doing the same for the multiple generations coming after them.

Generation X has unique characteristics that affect their relationship with life and money and the generations in front and behind them. These Gen X traits are reflected in many generation pseudonyms. Many are relevant to the discussions in this book; here are four that are affecting their and their family's finances:

TRAITS OF GENERATION X

The Latchkey Kids • The Experiment Generation • The Sandwich Generation • The Forgotten Generation

---

For all the rave about how artificial intelligence will change the world, emotional intelligence is shaping the world. Each generation's natural inclination is to hopefully instill enough in the next generation for them to do better than their predecessors and advance the human condition for themselves. Absent egregious intentional acts by mischievous parents and social systems, most folks within their generation go about this mission with good intentions, doing their best with the ability, information, resources, and skills available to them at the time.

Generations experience inherent strengths and weaknesses from their predecessors and attempt to make adjustments within themselves and across to the next. Some lessons and pearls of wisdom are fantastic carry-forwards, whereas others are best left behind; some are carried forward but shouldn't be, and others were not corrected when they should have been.

The holistic approach to life and money – bridging the current and future selves while living fully now and securing a future with compassion without shame or guilt, all while having the audacity to live abundantly and aspirationally – seems too much like a "pink cloud," temporary feelings of heightened confidence, euphoria, elation, or joy directly following a stage of change. You can't do all of that, can you? No, there isn't a perfect solution. However, there are healthy approaches that can help produce and sustain your intended outcomes.

The previous chapters unpack the LMB philosophy that contains The Six-A Financial Harmony System, the Humanity of Money, and the Five-Point Planning Process to wholly build, discover, and live your *Wealth in the Keys of Life* and find financial harmony. Let's walk through time to understand better what previous generations have been through, their struggles, contributions to advancing the next, and what that means to why Generation X is uniquely positioned to make a difference in the lives and finances of those to come. Gen X can shape and support cross-generationally but must put their holistic oxygen masks on first.

THE SILENT GENERATION[101,102]

(1928–1945)

The Silent Generation, before the Boomers, were survivors of the Depression Era and scarcity. The Stock Market Crash of 1929, including the infamous Black Tuesday, and failed economic and social policy led to zero-sum games among the populace. This developed a "scarcity of resources" mentality, not only outside the household affecting aspirations and expressions but inside the household, where vulnerable communications between spouses, parents, and young or adult children were scant or perhaps prohibited.

Much energy was dedicated to surviving. Surviving was considered thriving, not surviving *through to* thrive. The practice of most well-being dimensions was *seen, not heard* – being allowed a conforming physical presence but lacking the liberty or space to speak first, freely, or openly. There was no space for vulnerability, compassion, empathy, or understanding. Stacking on top of scarcity, these traumas were exacerbated by social, domestic, and world wars. An extreme trade-off for protecting against scarcity by sacrificing some well-being to promote a sense of safety, this generation is fantastic at delayed gratification and high savings rates for the future.

Everything comes with a cost. For every unit of well-being sacrificed by the Silent Generation, they laid foundations that the next generation built upon. Sensing the social and economic drags on the greater good and individual well-being, the Silent Generation began planting seeds such as the establishment of Social Security in 1935 with the intent of providing guaranteed government payment to replace a fractional share of a person's income during retirement, helping protect the elderly from abject poverty during old age – a government pension. The Silent and Boomer Generations will become the greatest benefactors of the Social Security retirement program, a public pension program.

THE BOOMER GENERATION[103]

(1946–1964)

The Boomer Generation is a post–World War II generation that experienced new senses of booms and their share of traumatic busts. Part of the boom was the economic expansion and recovery from World War II, record-level birthrates, accelerated cultural expressions of self and the arts, thriving higher education buoyed by accessible costs, GI Bills, other support opportunities, and small steps in social advancements. That said, for every seeming boom of the Boomer generation, there were some traumatic busts, such as the Vietnam War, government mistrust, and social inequality, including racial, gender, marital, sexual, and economic inequality. Depending on which side you had access to, the boom or bust side of the Boomer generations, the financial and Humanity of Money scripts, advances, or barriers carried over to the next generation. As discussed in previous chapters, living transfers of human and financial capital are just as important as any potential post-life financial bequest.

For those with access to the boom, Boomers used the savings mentality from their Silent Generation predecessors. They also carried over, although improved, still incomplete communication, vulnerability, and compassion skills among themselves, their spouses, young and adult children, and parents. Boomers made good use of their access to higher education with solid blue-collar or upper-white-collar jobs. They had more well-being than previous generations because of the previous environment of external strife and internal self-expression of shame. Professionally, they had faith in company loyalty and access to public and private pensions as part of their retirement plans.

The first private company pension plan was introduced in 1875 by American Express, which took instruction from the first versions of pensions from the Navy.[104] The most beneficial pension plans became prominent until after the 1950s through public and private pensions. Pensions are guaranteed income where employees defer a portion of their annual salary back to the employer. The employer collects from each employee, places the funds in one pot, and invests those funds to generate a return that can pay future income claims for retirees who have accumulated enough tenure at the company.

One takeaway is the bridge and balance between the current and future self; for Boomers, this bridge was still developing, approaching the elements of individual and household finances. Financial psychology and behavioral finance are in their infancy.

The concept of comprehensive financial planning for your personal finances consists of the government pension of Social Security retirement benefit, a potential company pension where the investment responsibility remains with the company and not the individual, and investing in the stock market happens with a wide information gap. For Boomers, they are undereducated financially and at risk of ill-intentioned investment professionals coupled with the emotional illogic of individual Humanity of Money and Life Money Balance exposure across their life course (see Introduction; LMB, Figure 1.2; HOM, Figure 1.3).

GENERATION X[105,106,107]

(1965–1980)

You may say you didn't come to read about and receive your Wealth in the Key of Life and read about a generational review. Well, this book intends to help people think and approach wealth and well-being differently – your Life Money Balance, those after you, and those you care for. Because of their life stage, generational position, mix of money life and social imprints, and advancements in financial education and psychology, Generation X has the opportunity to uniquely use the tools and philosophies in this book to change their course and live the life they want without shame, guilt, or regret.

After the economic adjustments of post-Vietnam and the energy crisis, the Silent Generation and Boomers gave birth to Generation X, who lay claim to growing up in the 30-year span of the 1970s, 1980s, and 1990s, including the glorious last year of disco, 1979.

In general, the 1980s and especially the 1990s saw upward mobility and social and systemic challenges, with Gen X becoming the first generation to face challenges to do financially better than their parents. Generation X struggled through stagflation in the 1970s (as young children growing up experiencing the financial effects of their parents' household), inflation in the 1980s, and a challenging workforce in the 2000s.

Then, there was wealth, some remnants of excessive greed. Remember the famous line in the movie *Wall Street*: "Greed is good!" This means that parents were busy pursuing professional endeavors for their households to prosper, which meant that the kids rode the bus to school after their parents went to work, rode it from school while their parents were at work, coming home to open the door with their latchkey, to wait for their parents to come home from work. This is how they got the moniker "latchkey kids."

Boomers *wanted* a better communication style with their children and tried to improve with the skills they acquired from their Silent Generation experiences. Still, with the self and professional advancements, one trade-off for household economics was a slowed rate of progress in talks about taboo areas such as money, sex, self-care, mental health, race, spousal, parent, and young and adult child communication without shame, guilt, or judgment.

You may remember "Just Say No," safe sex with condoms, the HIV and AIDS epidemics, Rodney King, the Berlin Wall, apartheid, parental warnings on music, MTV, and other events that signify that these discussions were coming to households. Still, the mass acceptance frameworks on how to have the discussions and tools to progress to and through thriving were in their infancy and began to find importance when Gen X began having children and working through their traumas in adulthood.

Because of the successful higher education and company blueprint from the Boomers, a large majority of Generation X was encouraged to attend college. As a result, the cost of a college education became a top target for inflation, ranking in the top three with healthcare services across a two-decade span; the popularity of undergraduate education spawned the MBA craze, sparking a student loan rush as that value progressed from previous generations.

Higher education was assumed to contribute to greater advancement and income in the current professional system. For sections of society, that's true; higher education is a common thread for those with higher incomes and assets, including success as business owners. However, the cost of college has ballooned, and wages have not grown to outpace inflationary pressures in key household areas such as child care, housing, transportation, food, education services, health care, and other lifestyle areas. This is due to several macroeconomic and financial crises, such as the dot-com bust and 9/11, which hurt employees out the gate, then elongated wars and the 2008 financial crisis sparking multiple economic recessions, fueling much to be apprehensive about. Not all is doom and gloom. There were some financial and economic recovery years after the financial crisis. Still, with all these ingredients, there's a sense of psychological and financial fatigue – a state of mental, physical, and emotional burnout from lengthy financial stress and worry, leading to suboptimal, haphazard, or no decision-making about finances.

FINANCIAL FATIGUE

Mental, physical, and emotional exhaustion from overwhelming financial stress and worry leads to poor life and financial decisions.[108]

WHAT DOES GENERATIONAL INTELLIGENCE HAVE TO DO WITH THE MONEY?

If you are part of Gen X, you may know why you are called the Forgotten Generation. The "X" label of the generation seems fitting because it represents a sense of this generation's uncertain identity. Some unique characteristics are affiliated with Gen X.

COMMON GENERATION X CHARACTERISTICS
Resilience • Resourcefulness • Skepticism • Independence

Gen X are forgotten because for a long time, and still to this day, Gen X is not talked about enough. When the Millennial generation was first born, they were projected to be all the rave, being the largest generation by count in the United States. Sure, they have had unbridled access to the accelerated introduction of technologies, psychological dialogues, and financial education that Generation X had, which they are now passing on to Gen Z and Alpha. These *introductions*, navigations, and uses started and progressed with Gen X – but Gen X is overlooked in many ways.

THE EXPERIMENT GENERATION

Let's begin with Gen X being the "Experiment Generation" when it comes to building finances for the future. In previous generations, we spoke of saving and investing for the future self – retirement – where the investment, decision, and administration responsibility lies at the foot of institutions, whether they be public or private, promising a guaranteed income (pension plans, a type of defined benefit plan). Although the stock market was available to the general public, the information, financial education, access, and cost gaps were wide. The retirement emphasis was on the institution, not the individual.

Then came the introduction of the employer-based defined contribution plans (DC), one type of DC plan being the now-popular 401(k). You see, defined benefit pension plans are costly to firms to administer and fund; because of the Employee Retirement Income Savings Act of 1974 that set Internal Revenue Code (IRC) policy, the sponsors of these plans must annually fund them with enough money so the investment bucket is large enough to meet current and future predicted payouts. Additionally, firms accept investment risk by taking on the responsibility of selecting investments and managing the portfolio to help ensure the promise of payments. These annual funding and administration costs are expensive to firms, and they wanted a way to shift the retirement responsibility to individuals. Financial institutions were also interested in creating financial products that retail household investors could invest in over long periods of time.

The experiment was, and still is, can individuals make sound savings and investment decisions regarding their retirement? This question wasn't one that individuals willingly explored; it was thrust upon them. In the late 1970s, Congress passed the Revenue Act of 1978, creating IRC Section 401(k), which gave employees a tax-free option to defer types of compensation. A private sector benefits consultant, Ted Benna, now commonly called the "Godfather of the 401(k)," proposed a way for employers to create tax-advantaged employee savings accounts. In 1981, rules were issued for salary deferrals, and by 1983, most major companies offered 401(k) plans.[109,110] Popularity grew for three reasons.

Firstly, funding these retirement plans was cheaper and more predictable because the contribution was more defined than funding moving targets of future defined benefits, and individuals liked more control over their retirement investments. The thing is, just as Social Security retirement benefits weren't supposed to replace working income completely, Ted Benna himself has said 401(k)s are not the complete solution to retirement income due to bloated plan expenses, financial market risks, investment selection of the participant, and high fees of investment choices.[109,110]

This book does not say that you should not participate in your 401(k), nor am I saying that 401(k)s are scams. Taking advantage of employee matches and compounding the effects of tax-deferred growth can prove beneficial. An annual Fidelity report states that the 401(k) asset is central to employee-based millionaires, with the number of 401(k) millionaires contributing to their plans for 15 years or more steady on the rise during the 2000s, 2010s, and 2020s due to steady contributions and market conditions. The reported 401(k) drawbacks can be mitigated with the size of the plan, ethical plan sponsorship, higher self – financial education, and working with financial planners.

However, shifting complete retirement readiness responsibility to individuals has had a less than positive outcome because it lacks a holistic approach to finances that includes financial psychology, education, and literacy and well-being guided by fiduciary financial advice by financial institutions, employer sponsors, and financial advisors. It may take more policy nudges like the Secure Act 2.0, where there are automatic opt-ins to retirement plans and participants have to take action to opt-out.

You may ask, "If there are 401(k) millionaires and some of Gen X are doing decently, then why are we talking about a financial journey experiment gone wrong?" Gen X is worried across all income levels because of the Sandwich Generation and because they are the first to look at finances holistically. The financial experiment is not only about dollars but also about education engagement, alignment, uses, beliefs, and money fulfillment.

THE WEALTH TRANSFER[111]

Much has been written about the wealth transfer of the Boomer and Silent Generation to younger generations. However, sticking to the script, Gen X is mostly forgotten by younger generations, meaning Millennials, Gen Y, and Gen Z. Most of these wealth transfers must go through Gen X first. Cerulli reports that through 2045, $84 trillion will be transferred to younger generations, with $53 trillion moving from Boomers to Gen X.[112]

However, taking a holistic view of wealth transfer reveals that some of the financial psychology and personal finances across and within the generations will affect the impact of the transfer. Remember the lack of communication in the Boomer Generation among themselves, extending troubles from their Silent Generation parents?

The Cerulli study reveals that 35% of Boomers don't plan on discussing wealth transfer with the younger generation.[112] Early communication about legacy and finances is essential to effective and efficient wealth transfers, to carrying out legacy intentions, and to increasing impact on heirs, not to mention the emotional well-being of both generations.

There are a couple more factors to consider that will contribute to the cross-generational effect of the wealth transfer conversation. One is the transfer expectation. Generation X is worried about their retirement because they are sandwiched between two generations that may need them financially and emotionally. A financial windfall could help.

WEALTH TRANSFER STATISTICS[112,113,114]

$53 trillion from Boomers to Gen X
$15.8 trillion from Silent Generation
35% of Boomers say they don't plan on discussing the Wealth Transfer
70% say spending down will impact the amount of the transfer
68% of wealth transfer will come from households with at least $1 million in investable assets
6.9% of households have more than $1 million in investable assets

Much of the wealth transfer is to the 68% of households with $1 million of investable assets or more, and only 6.9% of households have that kind of wealth. Still, some transfer, large or small, is expected, and these conversations are essential to facilitate.[114] The same study reports that 57% of the respondents reported that having a financial professional would help with the transfer.[114] Still, if no talks are being had, the lack of communication affects the transfer transaction and sets up expectations for emotions to remain elevated.

Lastly, about expectation: people are living longer and healthier, whereas well-being and living fully are more readily accepted, which means more spending on retirement. Couple that with 40% of assets being used in the back half of retirement due to the high inflationary costs of healthcare, long-term care, and support services; reports show that 70% of Boomers say that spending down their assets will affect their transfer amount.[114]

Generation X, across all social and economic statuses, may not be coming into great amounts of sudden wealth. Even in higher-asset-level households, the transfer may be slower due to the use of trusts, where Boomers have more control of the distribution time period. The wealth transfer will have much to do with how Boomers and Gen X live out their utility preferences in the LMB Wheel and how they communicate about life and money cross-generationally.

GENERATION X IS WORRIED ABOUT RETIREMENT

Generation X is in a peculiar spot regarding their LMB journey because they are the Sandwich Generation. Gen X struggles to balance the family's finances and their current and future selves.

They are sandwiched between supporting the lifestyle and needs of adult children, taking advantage of their high incomes to fund their life

---

THE SANDWICH GENERATION
Adult Children • Lifestyle • Retirement • Aging Parents

---

stage vitality and live their lives fully, funding their future retirement to secure the life they want, and contending with aging parent care or at least getting prepared for doing so.

Gen X is not confident about retirement. One study by Goldman Sachs revealed that 45% say they are behind on retirement savings, and only 55% say they have personalized financial plans, which stereotypically places them as generational individuals and skeptics.[115]

Moreover, Gen X possesses the highest average school loan account balances among the generations at $48,733, the highest median income at $101,500,[116,117] and the highest reports of financial trauma, where 74% of Gen X feel objective or subjective emotional distress from relationships with money past or present.[118] A Schwab study conducted in 2023 revealed that folks felt that they need at least $2.2 million of net worth, not including real estate, to feel wealthy; only 41% of Gen X feel wealthy, and they have an average of $410,000 net worth.[119] Lastly, the Goldman study tells us that only 12% of Gen X intend to leave an inheritance.[115]

WHAT DOES THIS ENTIRE CHAPTER MEAN TO YOU AS A GEN XER AND TO YOUR LIFE, FINANCES, AND FUTURE?

How can you live fully now and secure retirement confidently? What is your *Wealth in the Key of Life*? How can you change the course of your life to live abundantly and aspirationally, as well as the generations coming up behind you, and give grace to the generations before you?

It's all in the LMB Wheel, the Six-A Financial Harmony System, and the Humanity of Money. You are at the peak life stage to grab hold of your vital years and swim the Sea of C's, gaining confidence, control, and clarity. You can also use the wisdom from the culmination of Teas of Money and the Teas of Life to soothe generational transfers of emotion, wisdom, short-comings, experiences, values, cultures, communications, wishes, and finances to bridge and build better relationships with money, self, spouses, family, and future. It seems like a tall order, but being sandwiched is a tall order anyway, and each generation has its sacrifices and gems to leave behind. Put your oxygen mask on first; give yourself grace and practice self-care. Believe in living an abundant life the way you define it. Then, build better bridges to help navigate your money life better than the ways of the past and improve on the present.

KEY TAKEAWAYS

- For all the rave about how artificial intelligence will change the world, emotional intelligence is shaping the world.
- Right now, one generation uniquely captures the cross-generational transition in how they, their families, and society handle life and money; that's Generation X (Gen X).
- Gen X are sandwiched between supporting the lifestyle and needs of adult children, taking advantage of their high incomes to fund their life stage vitality and live their lives fully, and funding their future retirement.
- Gen X is worried across all income levels. The financial experiment is not only about dollars but also about education engagement, alignment, uses, beliefs, and money fulfillment.

Journal to Find Your Financial Harmony

Feelings + Finances helps your Finances Flourish. Take time to reflect on the takeaways in this chapter. Enjoy your time and journal only what connects with you most. Any findings during your journaling discovery will help you activate the Five-Point Life Planning Process.

- What life and money themes in this chapter speak specifically to your journey?
- Can you identify opportunities in your feelings and finances to align your life and money aspirations better, giving your money assignments to achieve the life you want?
- Were there any messages in the chapter that helped you:
  - Shake social money stigmas.
  - Release or address money anxiety, judgment, or shame.
  - Move toward better security and understanding of your finances.
  - Find more contentment or fulfillment or want to find some.
  - Discover or improve your relationship with money.
- Scan the Life Money Balance® Wheel, the Six-A-Alignment System™, and the Humanity of Money™. Did content in the chapter help you see yourself in a life stage, season, preference, domain, aspiration, money goal, or mindset?

Journaling Page

_____

_____

_____

_____

_____

_____

_____

_____

_____

_____

_____

_____

_____

_____

_____

CONCLUSION
YOUR KEYS TO HOLISTIC WEALTH

I first started on my transformation journey in 2016, but unknowingly, I began in 2012 in financial bankruptcy, a few years before a spirit bankruptcy, then a breakthrough to balance – letting life lead my money life and money and grabbing hold of my aspirational life. I didn't know I'd be writing a book that could help bring about change in the lives of others. I hope the personal stories and transformational change that I experienced, coupled with the professional knowledge I have accumulated in the financial planning, financial psychology, and financial therapy world as well as academia, have provided a different perspective and a new permission to have a unique and personal relationship with your money. Hopefully, some of these perspectives resonate with your inner vision. Then, your money can fund your preferences for life with the aspirations you so boldly deserve because you are worthy of living in abundance.

Many personal finance books are full of rigid technical strategies guiding you through types of retirement accounts, trusts, life insurance, complex estate planning and protection mechanisms, tax planning strategies, and so on. I'm capable of delivering such a book – and at Concurrent Financial Planning, we provide clients with comprehensive financial planning strategies to help them achieve their life and financial goals. If you're interested in those types of books, they are good reads, and I suggest you read them. The intention of this book is different; it is to help people like you have a different partnership with money, independent of social norms, that is fulfilling. I want to help you find harmony and create *Wealth in the Key of Life*. What does that mean?

Life is a continuum, a movie of integrated scenes and a song of harmonious notes. In life and financial terms, both happen across a life cycle, where money accumulation and decumulation occur. In life, there are moments of challenge and moments to celebrate. Our money is different in each life stage, and so is our purpose and preference during these stages. Our life is integrated into our ideal versions of our current and future selves, trying to maximize the best versions of ourselves across the domains of life. When you find *Wealth in the Key of Life* and the financial harmony of wealth and well-being, using LMB will help with integrated life stage well-being. LMB helps with your financial life planning in the areas you value most across LCU, MPU, and LSU, blending your person, purpose, process, and plan to achieve prosperity.

Having a framework of a process to experience and see through to transformation is the payoff to your life and finances flourishing and the gift of the Six-A Financial Harmony System. When you decide to come out of the darkness to the light of your life and finances, whether it be from a challenging point or a champion point, and you courageously decide to have the willingness to change, boldly create your life design, and go after your aspirational life, that's when your finances begin to prosper. This system applies to everyone across the socioeconomic spectrum; it is designed to meet you where you are and help you get where you want to go.

The first step is admitting where you are, and this is where you begin to feel the restrictive weight off your shoulders. The first day of the Six-A Financial Harmony System is the emotional Honest Self-Audit, or eHSA. It's the honest account of oneself. After you admit where you are, you acknowledge how you feel about the past, present, and future. This is where you meditate, reflect, and process your feelings to prepare your spirit and finances for a healthier state in which to take action. When you're in the action stage, you are preparing to leave the gate and arrive at the runway to take flight. Action begins with the belief that you are worthy of living in abundance and that you can achieve the aspirations that you set forth. Flourishing is for you!

The second set of the Six-A Financial Harmony System begins the fun part. Aligning your money values is essential because you're clearing out any conditional social norms, internal conditions, or beliefs that may have been influenced by information or value systems that are not yours. Here, you are auditing your life and money values, investigating objective information, and preparing to apply it to your aspirational life. Too often, there are social stigmas regarding money values, but this is an excellent place to shake off the shackles of social seams and switch those to tailored successes. Next, you have cleared the pathway of life and money alignment. You are giving your money assignments because you will identify your aspirations and commit energy and dollars to make those happen on your own terms, blocking out all the noise. Having intrinsic aspirations is the most important part of achieving the life that you want because they are the connective glue that will keep you bound to your financial life plan. Your aspirations will keep your motivations and spirits high when life and money are going well, remind you of purpose and encourage you in periods of challenge, and bring you back on course when your directional compass may stray.

Lastly, the joy you experience when you achieve your financial milestones is the magic of the transformational experience. You will reach a moment where "more" becomes "more than enough" in a dollar sense, but you will also consistently achieve some purposeful milestone of life and realize a return on life. Your first transformational experience with the LMB process will be your most memorable and likely have the greatest effect. The others will also have joy; you can use those to compound on the first. Creating *Wealth in the Key of Life* as you define it and finally finding financial harmony between your wealth and well-being, using the LMB wheel, is best served with the financial planning process. A trusted financial planning professional will connect with your life and deliver financial advice you can see and value.

Hopefully, in the chapters of this book, there is a question that I helped answer for you or helped shed light upon. Too often, money is taboo. Too often, we are stuck and do not forgive ourselves. Too often, we don't adhere to a process to investigate our internal selves, release ourselves from the past, and bring ourselves to the present. There's too much shame, too much stigma. There's too much highbrow, too much judgment on lifestyle preferences, and too many *shoulds* and *should nots* regarding what we value in our identities – what categories in the LMB we invest our money in and across what life stages. Frankly, it's nobody's business. What is important is that you care for your and your family's well-being and invest your dollars in a way that maximizes your utility for your household with unbiased information that is soundly grounded in empirical or theoretical research and interpreted with integrity so you can make the best decisions that serve your best interest.

Life is an interpretive art. So is money. As I've mentioned many times in this book, life and money are partners. Partnerships have soul, and music moves the soul. That's why, when you are building your *Wealth in the Key of Life*, you are building wealth and well-being. You are using your wealth dollars to fund the state of well-being you want to be in using your 12 notes to arrange your song. We know that every song is different; navigating through high notes, low notes, and vocal chords, harmony flows like music.

FURTHER READING

1. Delle Fave, A. (2014). *"Harmony" In Encyclopedia of Quality of Life and Well-Being Research*, edited by A. C. Michalos. Springer, Dordrecht. https://doi.org/10.1007/978-94-007-0753-5_1231.
2. Consumer Financial Protection Bureau (2015). *Financial Well-Being: The Goal of Financial Education*. https://files.consumerfinance.gov/f/201501_cfpb_report_financial-well-being.pdf.
3. World Health Organization. 2024. Health and Well-Being. Accessed September 9, 2024. https://www.who.int/data/gho/data/major-themes/health-and-well-being.
4. Bertalanffy, L. (1972). "The History and Status of General Systems Theory." *Academy of Management Journal* 15 (4): 407–426.
5. Psychology Today (2022). "Person-Centered Therapy." Accessed September 9, 2024. https://www.psychologytoday.com/us/therapy-types/person-centered-therapy.
6. Cherry, K. (2023). "What Motivation Theory Can Tell Us about Human Behavior." Verywell Mind. https://www.verywellmind.com/theories-of-motivation-2795720.
7. Pindyck, R. S., and D. L. Rubinfeld (2018). *Microeconomics* (9th edition). London: Pearson.
8. Bryant, W. K., and C. D. Zick. (2006). *The Economic Organization of the Household* (2nd ed.). New York: Cambridge University Press. https://doi.org/10.1017/CBO9780511754395.

9. Francisco Jose Ricardo Projects, "Quincy's 36 Seconds on the 12 Musical Notes," YouTube video, 0:26, July 12, 2019, https://www.youtube.com/watch?v=n7jBa4YcedI.

10. Freiman, S. (2016, September 29). "Decades Later, 'Songs in the Key of Life' Is as Fresh as Ever." CultureSonar. https://www.culturesonar.com/songs-in-the-key-of-life-40th-anniversary/.

11. Saad, L. (2023, May 18). "Americans Remain Discouraged about Personal Finances." Gallup. https://news.gallup.com/poll/506012/americans-remain-discouraged-personal-finances.aspx.

12. Lebow, H. I. (2022, June 24). "What are the 5 Types of Avoidance Behavior?" PsychCentral. https://psychcentral.com/health/types-of-avoidance-behavior#cognitive.

13. YMW Advisors (2020). "Your Money Script." Your Mental Wealth Advisors. https://www.yourmentalwealthadvisors.com/our-process/your-money-script/#:~:text=Money%20avoidance%20can%20be%20associated,a%20sign%20of%20Money%20Avoidance.

14. Prochaska, J. O., and J. C. Norcross (2018). *Systems of Psychotherapy: A Transtheoretical Analysis.* Oxford University Press.

15. Prochaska, J. O., and J. M. Prochaska (2016). *Changing to Thrive: Using the Stages of Change to Overcome the Top Threats to Your Health and Happiness.* Simon and Schuster.

16. Lurtz, M. (2021). "Helping Clients to Stop 'Thinking about it' (Contemplation) and Start 'Planning It' (Preparation)." Kitces. https://www.kitces.com/blog/contemplation-transtheoretical-model-doubt-delay-implement-change/.

17. Lurtz, M. (2021). "Helping Clients Change: From (Pre-)Contemplation to Implementation Action." Kitces. https://www.kitces.com/blog/pre-contemplation-stages-of-change-transtheoretical-model-changing-to-thrive/.

18. Irving, K. (2012). "The Financial Life Well-Lived: Psychological Benefits of Financial Planning." *Australasian Accounting, Business and Finance Journal* 6 (4): 47–59.

19. Irving, K., G. Gallery, N. Gallery, and C. Newton. (2011). "'I Can't Get No Satisfaction'... Or Can I?: A Study of Satisfaction with Financial Planning and Client Well-Being." *JASSA—The Finsia Journal of Applied Finance* 2: 36–44.

20. Uitti, J. (2022, September 20). "Behind the History and Meaning of the Term 'The Green Room.'" American Songwriter: The Craft of Music. https://americansongwriter.com/behind-the-history-and-meaning-of-the-term-the-green-room/.

21. Netsky, A. (2017, November 30). "The Tangle Origin Stories for the Term 'Green Room.'" OnStage Blog. https://www.onstageblog.com/columns/2017/11/30/the-tangled-origin-stories-for-the-term-green-room.

22. Schaper, D. (2023, January 10). "Traffic Congestion Got Much Worse in 2022 but Is Still below Pre-Pandemic Levels." NPR. https://www.npr.org/2023/01/10/1148205765/traffic-congestion-got-much-worse-in-2022-but-is-still-below-pre-pandemic-levels#:~:text=American%20drivers%2C%20on%20average%2C%20wasted%2051%20hours,costing%20$869%2C%20according%20to%20a%20new%20report.

23. Baikie, K. A., and K. Wilhelm (2005). "Emotional and Physical Health Benefits of Expressive Writing." *Advances in Psychiatric Treatment* 11 (5): 338–46. https://doi.org/10.1192/apt.11.5.338.

24. White, M., and D. Epston. (1990). *Narrative Means to Therapeutic Ends.* New York: W. W. Norton & Company.

25. Lada, B. (2024, June 4). "10 of the Hottest Cities in the US." AccuWeather. https://www.accuweather.com/en/weather-news/10-of-the-hottest-cities-in-the-us/432421.

26. "Annual Average Relative Humidity in US Cities." Current Results: Weather and Science Facts. Accessed September 11, 2024. https://www.currentresults.com/Weather/US/humidity-city-annual.php

27. Forbes, J. (2024, July 29). "The 10 Coldest States in the U.S., Ranked." Redfin. https://www.redfin.com/blog/coldest-states-in-the-us/.

28. American Psychological Association (2024). "What Is Cognitive Behavioral Therapy." Clinical Practice Guideline for the Treatment of Posttraumatic Stress Disorder. Accessed September 11, 2024. https://www.apa.org/ptsd-guideline/patients-and-families/cognitive-behavioral.

29. Aldredge, J. (2020, November 5). "The Fascinating History of the Clapperboard for Film and Video Production." PremiumBeat. https://www.premiumbeat.com/blog/clapperboard-for-film-and-video-production/.

30. Psychology Today Staff (2024). "Mindfulness: Present Moment Awareness." Psychology Today. Accessed September 11, 2024. https://www.psychologytoday.com/us/basics/mindfulness#:~:text=To%20live%20mindfully%20is%20to,body%20in%20an%20objective%20manner.

31. Bazley, W., C. Cuculiza, and K. Pisciotta (2021). "Being Present: The Influence of Mindfulness on Financial Decisions." *SSRN Electronical Journal* (January).

32. Wright, D. (2022, April 19). "How Does Mindfulness Impact How You Mange Your Money?" Yoga Journal. https://www.yogajournal.com/lifestyle/mindfulness-money-management/.

33. Ware, B. 2024. "Regrets of the Dying." Bronnie Ware. https://bronnieware .com/blog/regrets-of-the-dying/.

34. Ware, B. 2012. "The Top Five Regrets of the Dying: A Life Transformed by the Dearly Departing." *Proceedings (Baylor University Medical Center)* 25 (3): 299–300. https://www.ncbi.nlm.nih.gov/pmc/articles/PMC3377309/#:~:text=1)%20 %E2%80%9CI%20wish%20I',myself%20be%20happier%E2%80%9D%20(p.

35. "Stress in America 2023." (2023). American Psychological Association. Accessed September 11, 2024. https://www.apa.org/news/press/releases/ stress/2023/collective-trauma-recovery.

36. "Managing Your Stress in Touch Economic Times." (2010, November 1). American Psychological Association. Updated November 3, 2023. https:// www.apa.org/topics/money/economic-stress.

37. "Gratitude." (2018). APA Dictionary of Psychology. Accessed September 11, 2024. https://dictionary.apa.org/gratitude.

38. Emmons, R. A., and A. Mishra. (2011). "Why Gratitude Enhances Well-Being: What We Know, What We Need to Know." *Designing Positive Psychology: Taking Stock and Moving Forward* 248: 262.

39. Logan, A. (2022, December 6). "Can Expressing Gratitude Improve Your Mental, Physical Health?" Mayo Clinic Health System. Accessed September 11, 2024. https://www.mayoclinichealthsystem.org/hometown-health/speaking- of-health/can-expressing-gratitude-improve-health.

40. Psychology Today Staff (2024). "Solution-Focused Brief Therapy." Psychology Today. Accessed September 11, 2024. https://www.psychologytoday.com/us/ therapy-types/solution-focused-brief-therapy.

41. Halton, C. (2022). "Oprah Effect: What It Is, How It Works, Examples." Investopedia. https://www.investopedia.com/terms/o/oprah-effect.asp.

42. Ivanova, I. (2017, August 10). "Oprah's Greatest Product Hits. CBS News. https://www.cbsnews.com/news/oprah-winfreys-greatest-product-hits/.

43. Ward, A. F. (2013, July 16). "The Neuroscience of Everybody's Favorite Topic." Scientific American. https://www.scientificamerican.com/article/the- neuroscience-of-everybody-favorite-topic-themselves/.

44. CFP Board. (2022, January). *Guide to the 7-Step Financial Planning Process: A Case Study Illustration for Solo Practitioners.* https://www.cfp.net/-/media/ files/cfp-board/standards-and-ethics/compliance-resources/guide-to- financial-planning-process.pdf?la=en&hash=A8F02CC2451BE07E4FB05 DE009A64F68.

45. Klontz, B., B. T. Klontz, R. Kahler, and T. Klontz (2016). *Facilitating Financial health: Tools for Financial Planners, Coaches, and Therapists.* The National Underwriter Company.

46. Cherry, K. (2024). "Maslow's Hierarchy of Needs." Verywell Mind. Accessed September 11, 2024. https://www.verywellmind.com/what-is-maslows-hierarchy-of-needs-4136760.

47. Copley, L. (2024). "Hierarchy of Needs: A 2024 Take on Maslow's Findings." Positive Psychology. https://positivepsychology.com/hierarchy-of-needs/.

48. Wahome, C. (2022). "What Is Maslow's Hierarchy of Needs?" WebMD. https://www.webmd.com/mental-health/what-is-maslow-hierarchy-of-needs.

49. Setionago, B. (2023, November 30). "Income Boosts Self-Esteem More than Vice Versa, New Study Reveals." PsyPost. https://www.psypost.org/income-boosts-self-esteem-more-than-vice-versa-new-study-reveals/.

50. Chatterjee, S., M. Finke, and N. Harness. (2009). "Individual Wealth Management: Does Self-Esteem Matter?" *Journal of Applied Business & Economics* 10 (2).

51. Becker, G. S. (1976). *The Economic Approach to Human Behavior*. Chicago: The University of Chicago Press.

52. "Schwab Modern Wealth Survey, June 2023" (2023). Charles Schwab Corporation. Accessed September 11, 2024. https://www.aboutschwab.com/schwab-modern-wealth-survey-2023.

53. Van Boven, L., M. C. Campbell, and T. Gilovich. (2010). "Stigmatizing Materialism: On Stereotypes and Impressions of Materialistic and Experiential Pursuits." *Personality and Social Psychology Bulletin* 36 (4): 551–563.

54. Cherry, K. (2024, May 6). "What Are Aspirations?" Verywell Mind. https://www.verywellmind.com/what-are-aspirations-5200942#citation-1.

55. Berger, M. W. (2023, March 6). "Does More Money Correlate with Greater Happiness?" Penn Today. https://penntoday.upenn.edu/news/does-more-money-correlate-greater-happiness-Penn-Princeton-research.

56. Detrano, J. (2024). "Mapping Mental Health: Dr Swarbrick and the Eight Wellness Dimensions." Rutgers—New Brunswick Center of Alcohol and Substance Use Studies. https://alcoholstudies.rutgers.edu/mapping-mental-health-dr-swarbrick-the-eight-wellness-dimensions/.

57. "Eight Dimensions of Wellness." (2024). UC Davis Student Health and Counselin Services. Accessed September 11, 2024. https://shcs.ucdavis.edu/health-and-wellness/eight-dimensions-wellness.

58. Stoewen, D. L. (2017, August). "Dimensions of Wellness: Change Your Habits, Change Your Life." *The Canadian Veterinary Journal* 58 (8): 861–862. https://www.ncbi.nlm.nih.gov/pmc/articles/PMC5508938/.

59. Hill, P. L., N. A. Turiano, D. K. Mroczek, and A. L. Burrow (2016). "The Value of a Purposeful Life: Sense of Purpose Predicts Greater Income and Net Worth." *Journal of Research in Personality* 65: 38–42.

60. Park, L. E., Ward, D. E., and Naragon-Gainey, K. (2017). "It's All About the Money (for Some): Consequences of Financially Contingent Self-Worth." *Personality and Social Psychology Bulletin* 43 (5): 601–622. https://doi .org/10.1177/0146167216689080.

61. Dean, B. (2024) "Vitality." University of Pennsylvania—Authentic Happiness. Accessed September 11, 2024. https://www.authentichappiness.sas.upenn .edu/newsletters/authentichappinesscoaching/vitality#:~:text=In% 20both%20the%20physical%20and,actions%20have%20meaning%20and %20purpose.

62. Singh, J. (2022, January 21). "Arnold Schwarzenegger—'I Am Not a Self-Made Man.'" Lighthouse Global Community. Accessed September 11, 2024. https://www.lighthousecommunity.global/post/arnold-schwarzenegger-i-am-not-a-self-made-man.

63. Perry, T. (2022, September 1). "Arnold Schwarzenegger's Speech on Why He's Not a 'Self-Made Man' Shows Why We All Need Each Other." Upworthy. Accessed September 11, 2024. https://www.upworthy.com/arnold-schwarzenegger-s-speech-on-why-he-s-not-a-self-made-man-shows-why-we-all-need-each-other.

64. Cain, A. (2017, May 18). "'I Didn't Just Materialize out of Nowhere like the Terminator': Arnold Schwarzenegger Destroys the Idea of the Self-Made Man in His Speech to Grads." Business Insider. Accessed September 11, 2024. https://www .businessinsider.com/arnold-schwarzenegger-commencement-speech-2017-5.

65. "Our Approach: Self-Determination Theory." University of Rochester Medical Center. Accessed September 11, 2024. https://www.urmc.rochester.edu/ community-health/patient-care/self-determination-theory.aspx.

66. Moore, J. W. (2016). "What Is the Sense of Agency and Why Does It Matter?" *Frontiers in Psychology* 7: 1272.

67. "Financial Illiteracy Cost Americans $1,506 in 2023." (2024). National Financial Educators Council. Accessed September 11, 2024. https://www .financialeducatorscouncil.org/financial-illiteracy-costs/.

68. DeSteno, D., Y. Li, L. Dickens, and J. S. Lerner (2014). "Gratitude: A Tool for Reducing Economic Impatience." *Psychological Science* 25 (6): 1262–1267.

69. Wood, A. M., J. J. Froh, and A. W. A. Geraghty (2010). "Gratitude and Well-Being: A Review and Theoretical Integration." *Clinical Psychology Review* 30 (7): 890–905.

70. Locke, T. (2020, August 5). "How Bill Gates' Mom Helped Microsoft Get a Deal with IBM in 1980—and It Propelled the Company's Huge Success." CNBC Make It. Accessed September 11, 2024. https://www-cnbc-com.cdn.ampproject.org/v/s/www.cnbc.com/amp/2020/08/05/

how-bill-gates-mother-influenced-the-success-of-microsoft.html?
amp_gsa=1&amp_js_v=a9&usqp=mq331AQIUAKwASCAAgM%3D#
amp_tf=From%20%251%24s&aoh=17138140012565&csi=1&referrer=https
%3A%2F%2Fwww.google.com&ampshare=https%3A%2F%2Fwww.cnbc
.com%2F2020%2F08%2F05%2Fhow-bill-gates-mother-influenced-the-
success-of-microsoft.html.

71. ET Spotlight Team. (2008, June 26). "The Long and Successful Journey of Bill
Gates." The Economic Times. Accessed September 11, 2024. https://econom
ictimes.indiatimes.com/tech/ites/the-long-and-successful-journey-of-bill-
gates/articleshow/3166466.cms?from=mdr.

72. Lewis, R. F., and B. S. Walker. (2005). *Why Should White Guys Have All the
Fun?: How Reginald Lewis Created a Billion-dollar Business Empire.* Baltimore:
Black Classic Press.

73. Zimmer, B. (2010, December 16). "Acronym." *The New York Times Magazine.*
https://www.nytimes.com/2010/12/19/magazine/19FOB-onlanguage-t.html.

74. Shaw. N. (2022, January 10). "How Acronyms Hurt Efforts Towards Inclusion:
A Plea to Rethink How We Use Them." Medium. Accessed September 11, 2024.
https://medium.com/@natalie_shaw/how-acronyms-hurt-efforts-towards-
inclusion-a-plea-to-rethink-how-we-use-them-7233d8d58ec4.

75. Saavedra, J. (2024). "Aspirations: Definition, Examples, and Insights."
Berkeley Well-Being Institute. Accessed September 11, 2024. https://www
.berkeleywellbeing.com/aspirations.html#:~:text=Aspiration%20is
%20the%20driving%20feeling,to%20be%20a%20good%20father%
E2%80%9D.

76. De Visé, D. (2024, January 14). "A Middle-Age Millionaires' Row: Average
50-Something Now Has Net Worth over $1 Million." *USA Today.* https://www
.usatoday.com/story/money/2024/01/14/average-net-worth-1-
million-50-year-olds/72177890007/.

77. Kasser, T. (2016). "Materialistic Values and Goals." *Annual Review of
Psychology* 67: 489–514.

78. Stanley, T. J., and W. D. Danko. (1996). *The Millionaire Next Door: The
Surprising Secrets of America's Wealthy.* Government Institutes.

79. Johnson, H. D. (2023, November 30). "What Does It Mean to Be Frugal."
Bankrate. https://www.bankrate.com/banking/what-does-frugal-mean/.

80. "What Is Considered Mass Affluent Based off Income, Net Worth, and
Investable Assets" (2024, September 7). Financial Samurai. https://www
.financialsamurai.com/what-is-considered-mass-affluent-definition-based-
off-income-net-worth-investable-assets/.

81. Williams, C. (2023, September 12). "You've Heard of Being Rich, but How about Being Mass Affluent." Smart Asset. https://finance.yahoo.com/news/youve-heard-being-rich-being-130027891.html.

82. "The Two Levels of Rich: One of Which Doesn't Rely on Index Funds" (2024, August 27). Financial Samurai. Accessed September 11, 2024. https://www.financialsamurai.com/the-two-levels-of-rich/.

83. Corley, T. (2023, July 4). "I Spent 5 Years Interviewing 233 Millionaires—Here Are 5 Things They Never Waste Money On." CNBC Make It. https://www.cnbc.com/2023/07/04/i-asked-233-millionaires-what-they-stopped-wasting-money-on-after-they-got-rich.html#:~:text=3.,Outdoor%20tools%20and%20equipment.

84. Collins, C. (2024, May 19). "8 Things the Rich Spend Money on That Poor and Middle Class People Don't." GO Banking Rates. Accessed September 11, 2024. https://www.gobankingrates.com/money/wealth/things-rich-spend-money-on-that-poor-middle-class-do-not/?hyperlink_type=manual&utm_term=related_link_1&utm_campaign=1259652&utm_source=nasdaq.com&utm_content=2&utm_medium=rss.

85. Kolmar, C. (2022, November 17). "25+ Important Entrepreneur Statistics [2023]: What to Know Before You Start Business." Zippia. https://www.zippia.com/advice/entrepreneur-statistics/.

86. Houston, M. (2023, May 31). "The Impact of Mental Health on Business Owners." Forbes. https://www.forbes.com/sites/melissahouston/2023/05/31/the-impact-of-mental-health-on-business-owners/.

87. "Voltron: Defender of the Universe" (n.d.). Voltron Wiki. https://voltron.fandom.com/wiki/Category:Voltron:_Defender_of_the_Universe.

88. "PERMA Theory of Well-Being and PERMA Workshops." (2024). Penn Arts & Sciences Positive Psychology Center. https://ppc.sas.upenn.edu/learn-more/perma-theory-well-being-and-perma-workshops.

89. CFI Team. (2024). "PERMA Model." CFI. https://corporatefinanceinstitute.com/resources/management/perma-model/.

90. Asebedo, S. D., and M. C. Seay. (2015). "From Functioning to Flourishing: Applying Positive Psychology to Financial Planning." *Journal of Financial Planning* 28 (11): 50–58.

91. https://stayhipp.com/glossary/what-does-secure-the-bag-mean/

92. Coelho, P. (1998). *The Alchemist*. Harper San Francisco.

93. "Share of Americans Who Work with a Financial Advisor in 2022" (2024, March 7). Statista. https://www.statista.com/statistics/1176393/financial-advisor-usa/.

94. Deaton, H. (2022, December 8). "Americans without Advisors Are More Stressed. So Why Aren't They Engaging with Financial Professionals?" RIAIntel. https://www.riaintel.com/article/2azn9e8r9k3izwmsmcfls/ practice-management/americans-without-advisors-are-more-stressed-so-why-arent-they-engaging-with-financial-professionals#:~:text=Only%20 35%20percent%20of%20Americans,tasks%20that%20Americans%20find% 20overwhelming.

95. CFP Board (2022, January). "Guide to the 7-Step Financial Planning Process." https://www.cfp.net/-/media/files/cfp-board/standards-and-ethics/ compliance-resources/guide-to-financial-planning-process.pdf?la=en& hash=A8F02CC2451BE07E4FB05DE009A64F68.

96. "Investor Satisfaction with Full-Service Financial Advisors Crumbles as Markets Fall, J.D. Power Finds" (2023). J.D. Power. https://www.jdpower.com/ business/press-releases/2023-us-full-service-investor-satisfaction-study.

97. Buhrmann, J. (2023, July 18). "What Do Clients Want from Their Financial Advisor?" eMoney. https://emoneyadviser.com/blog/what-do-clients-want-from-their-financial-adviser.

98. "What Do Clients Want from Financial Advisors?" (2022, March 1). The American College. www.theamericancollege.edu/knowledge-hub/research/ what-do-clients-want-from-financial-advisers.

99. Cherry, P.D. (2024). "Why Advisers Need the Humanity of Money." *Journal of Financial Planning* 37 (5).

100. Bloomberg (2007, March 26). "Wealthy Households Show Independent Advisers the Money." Investment News. https://www.investmentnews.com/mutual-funds/ wealthy-households-show-independent-advisers-the-money/8171.

101. Wallenfeldt. J. (2024, August 16). "Silent Generation." Brittanica. https:// www.britannica.com/topic/Silent-Generation.

102. "The Silent Generation and Mental Health" (2024, May 4). Therapist.com. https://therapist.com/generations/silent-generation/.

103. "Baby Boomer: Definition, Age Range, Characteristics, and Impact" (2024, June 8). Investopedia. Accessed September 11, 2024. https://www.investopedia .com/terms/b/baby_boomer.asp.

104. "History of PBGC" (2024). Pension Benefit Guaranty Corporation. https://www.pbgc.gov/about/who-we-are/pg/history-of-pbgc#:~:text=In% 201875%2C%20the%20American%20Express,also%20began%20to% 20provide%20pensions.

105. Kagan, J. (2024, July 2). "Generation X (Gen X): Between Baby Boomers and Millenials." Investopedia. https://www.investopedia.com/terms/g/generation-x-genx.asp.

106. McKenna, A. (2024, September 4). "Generation X." Brittanica. https://www.britannica.com/topic/Generation-X.

107. Brock, C. (2024, January 12). "What Is Gen X?" The Motley Fool. https://www.fool.com/terms/g/gen-x/.

108. Adesakin, S. (2022, October 28). "Overcoming Financial Fatigue." Business Day. https://businessday.ng/life-arts/article/overcoming-financial-fatigue/.

109. Burleigh, E. (2024, May 2). "The 'Father of the 401(k)' Talks about the Death of Pensions, the Future of Retirement, and What Disturbs Him Most about His Own Creation." Yahoo! Finance. https://finance.yahoo.com/news/father-401-k-talks-death-120000677.html?guccounter=1&guce_referrer=aHR0cHM6Ly93d3cuZ29vZ2xlLmNvbS8&guce_referrer_sig=AQAAAM62wLiunlyFcb3LM83JnN4b-ZTnJW8YCKJT6JBy36a or6CBuu-S59L_4EU4k8EvpcLd5OQNnnKRxOQOGDKX-1kJOUSVYH Jwf0KLZktZe73uf-za_VLSwJYfBU0CCrMnJN5jIUsoHzoLu2W9 n4gAjcHQ9p0GDEYWhCFuWchizSjs.

110. Elkins, K. (2017, January 4). "A Brief History of the 401(k), Which Changed How Americans Retire." CNBC Make It. https://www.cnbc.com/2017/01/04/a-brief-history-of-the-401k-which-changed-how-americans-retire.html.

111. Kagan, J. (2024, July 2). "Generation X (Gen X): Between Baby Boomers and Millenials." Investopedia. https://www.investopedia.com/terms/g/generation-x-genx.asp.

112. "We Aren't Talking Enough about One Aspect of the Great Wealth Transfer" (2024, July 17). Milken Institute. https://milkeninstitute.org/article/wealth-transfer-baby-boomers.

113. Lisa, A. (2024, June 5). "Great Wealth Transfer: How Boomers Are Passing on Fortunes to Their Heirs." Yahoo! Finance. https://finance.yahoo.com/news/great-wealth-transfer-baby-boomers-110047810.html.

114. Jay, M. (2023, December 29). "The 'Wealth Transfer' from Boomers Won's Save Gen X and Millenials." NBC News. https://www.nbcnews.com/business/consumer/generational-wealth-transfer-baby-boomers-cant-save-gen-x-millennials-rcna128099.

115. Goldman Sachs Asset Management. (2024). *Diving Deeper into the Financial Vortex: The Generational Divide.* Goldman Sachs. https://www.gsam.com/content/dam/gsam/pdfs/common/en/public/articles/2024/am-retirement-survey-generational-report-2024.pdf?sa=n&rd=n.

116. Bareham, H. (2023, September 28). "Which Generation Has the Most Student Loan Debt?" Bankrate. https://www.bankrate.com/loans/student-loans/student-loan-debt-by-generation/#gen-z.

117. Hanson, M. (2023, September 24). "Student Loan Debt by Generation." Education Data Initiative. https://educationdata.org/student-loan-debt-by-generation.

118. Parker, K., and E. Patten. (2013, January 30). "The Sandwich Generation: Rising Financial Burdens for Middle-Aged Americans." Pew Research Center. https://www.pewresearch.org/social-trends/2013/01/30/the-sandwich-generation/.

119. Charles Schwab. Schwab Modern Wealth Survey: 2023 Findings. San Francisco, CA: Charles Schwab & Co., Inc., 2023.

INDEX